THE MONGREL METHOD

THE
MONGREL
METHOD

SALES & MARKETING
FOR THE
NEW BREED
OF BUYERS

STEVE DE MAMIEL

THE MONGREL METHOD
Sales and Marketing for the
New Breed of Buyers

ISBN   978-1-61961-619-6 *Paperback*
       978-1-61961-618-9 *Ebook*

LIONCREST
PUBLISHING

To Nick, Jacqueline, and Tom—three great reasons to get on and do it today. And to Rachel, who provided all the encouragement and support to do it today.

CONTENTS

DEFINITIONS

Samuel chasing the ball — by Jacqueline de Mamiel, age 11

In·tent: Intention or purpose. An anticipated outcome that is intended or that guides your planned actions. In marketing, it's looking at the actions (purchases, activity, research) that show the client is moving toward a solution.

Met·a·phor: A figure of speech that refers, for rhetorical effect, to one thing by mentioning another thing. It may provide clarity or identify hidden similarities between two ideas. Each chapter of this book opens with a story about Sam that is a metaphor for a sales or marketing idea.

Meth·od: Orderliness of thought or behavior; systematic planning or action.

Mon·grel: Often used to describe a mix of dog breeds. Any cross between different types of animals or things.

Mongrel Method: A mix of sales and marketing plus the new way to plan and understand the client's intent.

Samuel de Mamiel: The mongrel mutt that quietly excelled in sales and marketing by quickly establishing a rapport and trust with clients while lying around vineyards and pushing soggy balls at them.

INTRODUCTION

Sam was the family mutt. He was purchased for twenty dollars. He tagged along with me everywhere I went and developed quite a name for himself in the process. His favorite outings were to my weekend jobs at the vineyards I worked for in Western Australia. Over the years, he became part of the daily fabric at those vineyards and everywhere else he went.

If I was in the cellar sales, the retail shop in the front of the winery, Sam manned the front of the shop, greeting visitors with an enthusiastic tail wag and a slobbery smile. He saw any newcomer as a potential playmate, someone to throw his ball for him or offer a scratch behind the ears. On the rare occasions his ball was confiscated or lost, he went and found a stick or something else to fetch. His excitement was infectious, and there wasn't a soul who didn't warm to him.

He taught me and those around him a lot about relationships and behavior. He embodied many of the characteristics that most humans try to emulate: determination, loyalty, friendliness, protectiveness, and always a thirst for adventure.

I often share stories about Sam in my sales and marketing training sessions because he was so likeable. I use the stories as metaphors for salespeople's behaviors. Sam often behaved in a way that salespeople do, and I think there are valuable things to be learned from him. His memory lives on, and it lives large in those stories. Over time, I've discovered that any tale involving Sam sticks in people's minds. People are able to relate to him and his endearing personality. Much of his behavior—his persistence and his powers of persuasion—directly relates to the methods I teach. He provides a fresh perspective, which makes it easy for my students to retain and apply the principles I share to their own sales and marketing arsenal.

WHY THIS BOOK?

It's no secret the world is full of sales and marketing books. *The Mongrel Method* is different. Based on the techniques and principles I've gathered over twenty years in the ever-evolving IT sector, I've seen the requirements for sales and marketing teams shift even faster than the technology. The world has changed quickly, and with it so has client behavior.

This book will clearly define modern sales and marketing responsibilities, as well as provide guidance on how to interact with and engage contemporary clients. Each chapter starts with a story about Sam and is followed by an explanation of a modern sales or marketing concept and how to best utilize it with today's clients. Metaphors are a powerful way to get people to retain ideas, and Sam has given me no shortage of stories and anecdotes to share with people over the years. The chapters end with action steps, called "Best in Show," which represent the best, applicable practices to implement into your own sales and marketing method. My intention is to challenge professionals to approach clients in a new way that results in long-lasting, trusting relationships.

Salespeople are no longer responsible for educating or persuading clients to buy a product or service. The Internet has taken care of that legwork. Clients are out there educating themselves, researching the products or services they need, and forming their own opinions. They're talking to their friends and colleagues about the best brands, they're following the top influencers on social media, and they're listening to the online conversations.

The sheer volume of published information in the modern era is staggering. Buying opinions and brand biases are established long before a salesperson has direct engagement with a client. Clients come to the table with advanced product knowledge. They largely engage with the salesperson when they are more than 50 percent of the way through the decision process. As a result, sales cycles are shorter and clients start the conversation with fixed ideas about what they need. The salesperson's role is now one of "decision enabler."

What does this mean for today's sales and marketing teams, and how can they capture the interest and dollars of the modern consumer? More than ever before, it means sales must work hand in hand with marketing.

THE NEW WORLD OF SALES AND MARKETING

In most industries, anyone who has more than fifteen years of experience is considered to know their stuff. In sales and marketing, however, if you have more than ten years of experience, it is of limited value.

Given that salespeople are an expensive resource, business owners need to address their attention toward how and in what capacity their sales team is best utilized. It's not just about covering their base salary anymore; it's about the company car, the cell phone bill, and the laptop. The best use of a salesperson's time is no longer spent educating the clients. That activity has shifted and is more effectively executed by marketing. Furthermore, the client will not accept education from a salesperson. Independent, unbiased information is widely available, as is access to other clients' experiences.

Marketing needs to take ownership of the client's early research and help to shape their opinions of the company. Salespeople have not been removed from the equation, but they have taken on an entirely different role. Their role must encompass elements of project management and business analysis, more so today than in the past. Therefore, the sales approach needs to be entirely different as well. In working with the client to build a business case, or project plan, they are actually qualifying the opportunity.

The sales conversation should start with unearthing the client's issues or pain points. What are your clients trying to move toward and/or away from? The function of sales is to enable decision-making. A salesperson needs to establish trust and build rapport while getting the client to articulate their issue. If it turns out the client needs more information to define the solution, they need to be shifted back over to marketing.

In the past, marketing involved taking a half-educated guess, at best. Due to the rise of Facebook, and online user behavior tools such as Google Analytics, there is no more guessing. Marketing's role has shifted from an art to a science with joint accountability for results with sales. We have the resources to know what is going on online in real time, all the time. We can directly pinpoint where the clients are and what they're engaging in.

Whereas marketing used to focus on market segmentation, demographics, or psychographics, today it's about understanding user data. In the early stages of this new era, marketing departments created client personas. Now we know we must make decisions according to what people are doing online and identify the client's intent. What is leading, motivating, and driving the client? What new or additional information do they need to make a decision?

Successfully navigating the new sales and marketing paradigm means meeting the clients where they are. It allows teams to develop better and stronger connections with their clients because they are involved and actively engaged with them, and they better understand what their needs are. Participation in and promotion of online groups helps to build and create a brand or company reputation. To be perceived as a thought leader, you must be a part of the conversation, if not even directing it. Respect leads to trust, which leads to stronger relationships.

Understanding company structure is also critical in today's sales environment. No one single person is the designated decision maker any more. In most organizations, a group of people makes the purchasing decisions; therefore, singling just one person out to speak to could easily backfire. Multiple stakeholders means there might be separate decision criteria, which is critical information when trying to appeal to a collective.

My goal in writing this book is to help modern sales and marketing teams build sustainable relationships with their prospective and current clients. Today's selling is centered in reaching a mutual agreement. There needs be something worth moving forward on together; the sale needs to make sense from both sides of the coin. The minute things begin to feel one-sided or forced, the clients will become defensive and disengage.

The lessons Sam taught me about life are timeless. One of the many things he showed me was that no one wants to play fetch alone. People want to engage and interact; they want to work with people who care about them, respect them, and trust them. Above all, they want to work with people who are genuinely enthusiastic and passionate.

To avoid an extended game of cat and mouse—or dog and ball—meet your clients where they are. Physically, they are online; mentally, they are halfway through the buying cycle by the time you speak to them. Get to the heart of their issues, and let them know how you can solve them. In other words, *stop selling and start solving.*

BUYING CYCLE

Old vs. New Buying Journey

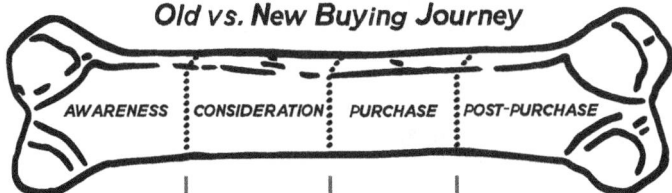

AWARENESS	CONSIDERATION	PURCHASE	POST-PURCHASE
Sales Prospecting / Education	Sales Qualifying and Competitive Bidding	Sales handover to technical or PM team	Sales of add-ons by sales team through ad hoc sales calls

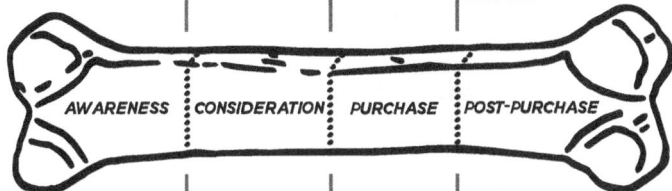

AWARENESS	CONSIDERATION	PURCHASE	POST-PURCHASE
-Marketing capture and nurture leads -Marketing helps customer define issue and educates on solution	-Marketing hands over qualified lead to sales -Sales helps build business case	-Sales works with and transitions to technical or PM team -Sales directly involve in PM. Plan just prior to purchase decision	-Sales and Marketing continue communication -Customer begins to contribute to the community -Marketing discovers product improvement opportunities

CHAPTERS	CHAPTERS	CHAPTERS	CHAPTERS
∨	∨	∨	∨
Like a dog with a phone	Poodles Bite Too Going to the Vet Who Will Feed the Dog? Stop Playing Fetch	How Much Is That Doggy? In the Dog House It's Time to Stop Barking	Roam In Packs

CHAPTER 1

LIKE A DOG WITH A PHONE

Like most dogs, the minute Sam got a new bone, it was the only thing he could focus on. He put his whole body into the attention he gave it, crouching over the bone protectively, head down, completely oblivious to the outside world. If someone interrupted him while he was gnawing, Sam did not respond favorably. Teeth gnarled, he gave off a guttural groan that said, "Get away from me and my bone. I am busy and I might bite you." His message came through loud and clear.

While the bone was still fresh, it never left Sam's vicinity. He kept tabs on it the way someone would with a brand-new phone. He carted it around with him everywhere and had specific spots mapped out where he would pause and give it some focused attention. He circled the area, chose the precise spot he had in mind, set the bone down gingerly, gave it some licks for good measure, a few chews, and picked it up in his teeth to repeat the entire process all over again.

THE MOBILE REALITY

The way Sam was with a bone reminds me of how most people—especially salespeople—are with their cell phones. The phones never leave their hands. They walk around hunched over it phones, pecking at the keyboard, and swiping at their apps. Reports vary on how often people check their phones, but the numbers range anywhere from every hour to eighty-five times a day.

We are all just like Sam was with his bones when it comes to our phones: tireless. The bone/phone is the focal point of our existence, on a truly primal level. Beware the person who tries to come between a dog and his bone or someone with her phone. The teeth come out and the growling starts, because the phone is the bone in the center of our respective universes.

In the last decade, people have started turning more and more toward their mobile phones when they're looking for information. Our handheld computers have replaced the desktop because of the immediacy they afford, but most marketing departments haven't caught up. There is an urgent need for marketing to adjust their strategic initiatives by acknowledging that mobile offers the number-one opportunity to share content, boost client engagement, and be a part of the online conversation.

Having a fancy website is not enough to attract, interact with, and retain clients. It's not about making phone calls, snail-mail campaigns, or heavy-stock business cards. It's about text and instant messaging, mobile friendly websites, and social media management through the phone. It cannot be an afterthought or an add-on. An effective marketing strategy begins with mobile.

The daily workplace in most mature markets is still heavily centered around the desktop, which is one reason marketing has been slow to catch up. Even with the rise of telecommuting, the "norm" still involves people going into an office, firing up a laptop or a desktop, and settling into their work for the day. Those who have traditional, nine-to-five office jobs spend a considerable amount of time in front of their computer screens, but almost everyone with a smartphone uses it constantly.

The big push toward mobile began in Asia where physical space is a rare luxury, but Internet access is not. Companies such as Samsung and Apple were the smartphone pioneers, and they continue to play a big role in the cell phone market. A number of developing markets in Africa and Asia bypassed the desktop computer phenomenon altogether and went straight to mobile devices and infrastructure. They started out with Internet access on their mobile devices. Cell phones have quickly become the primary means of connecting with the world, including people sitting right in front of you. Anyone with a teenager can easily relate.

Although many marketing professionals behave similarly in their personal lives, for some inexplicable reason the same behavior doesn't translate over to their business planning. Most people, *especially marketers*, are distrustful of companies that don't have an online presence or disclose pricing information. Why would they not apply the same logic to the companies they work for? The shift toward mobile is upon us, and marketing needs to catch up.

Google has been a significant driver in the push toward mobile. In April 2015, it started ranking mobile-friendly sites. Sites with enhanced mobile readability get consistently higher rankings. The results of their experiments are widely published, and they've promoted a new "open standard" called Accelerated Mobile Pages (AMP) on how websites should be written for mobile optimization. As businesses start to monitor their rankings and make internal decisions that boost their visibility, mobile adaptability will inevitably become the new normal.

CONSUMER HABITS

The very first thing people do at the beginning of each day is check their phones. It starts with the alarm, which more often than not is set through an app. As they reach over to hit snooze, or turn the alarm off, they start checking up on what they've missed overnight: e-mails, texts, Facebook and Instagram posts, top news stories, stock prices, sports scores, and everything else that is of interest to them.

Our days begin and end with the phone, and so should a sound marketing plan. The phone is no longer about making calls. People don't even answer their phones any more, unless they know who is calling. Call response rates have dropped from about 40 percent in the 1990s to 9 percent today. A 2016 article in *Forbes* said that as many as 97 percent of business calls go unanswered; therefore, relationship development must come first before the phone is answered.* Given those alarming numbers, businesses that have not built trust with the prospective client put their sales teams in a difficult position, because no one is going to take your call without knowing who you are.

The phone is a device to gather information and solve problems, and it's with us all day, every day. Mobile allows us to make immediate, low-involvement decisions with high frequency. People have come to expect access to whatever they want in just one click. Businesses that overcomplicate that process for the client, by adding more steps or click-throughs, are only alienating themselves. They're starting from behind, and their clients will go elsewhere, and fast.

If the client is searching for information regarding a high-involvement decision, he may want to communicate with someone about it directly. The ability to use the same device that his search was conducted on to call, text, or

* Jonjie Sena, "Consumers Don't Trust Phone Calls from Businesses: Here's How to Restore Their Faith," *Forbes*, September 7, 2016, http://www.forbes.com/sites/neustar/2016/09/07/consumers-dont-trust-phone-calls-from-businesses-heres-how-to-restore-their-faith/#270accea23d2.

chat with a person at the company removes one more step for the client. Plus, he is coming to the phone, text, or chat informed and ready to go.

Although desktop websites have become secondary to mobile marketing, they still have a place in the marketing matrix. It's much easier to address complicated issues on a larger screen. When there is a high-involvement decision on the line, with seven or more factors at play, desktop plays a key role. For example, if someone is planning to buy a car or a house, or even planning a holiday, they need to do more research than they would if they were buying a pair of shoes. Desktop sites are appropriate for the elements of marketing that require specific, text-heavy detail and high-impact visuals and video. Once they have examined the information, the consumer will make the decision to reach for the phone or not.

SAMUEL SAYS: MARKETING BEGINS WITH MOBILE.

HOW TO GET IN THE GAME

Given the wide availability of peer and product reviews, as well as general online discussions around specific solutions, more than ever, clients are out there educating themselves. If marketers are on their game, they're participating in those conversations, establishing trust, and co-opting support from opinion leaders. They're contributing to the consumers' education as well as the formation of their beliefs and biases. They're providing the clients with the appropriate amount of information and the right resources, so when a client is ready to pick up the phone, he's already halfway to a buying decision.

In the past, consumers began with somewhere between six and ten organizations that might be able to provide them with a solution. They engaged with all of them, gathered information, became better educated, and then started to whittle down their options.

The process is far simpler and less time-consuming now. Depending on what type of solution someone is looking for, they might easily look at a few industry forums, visit LinkedIn groups to see what they're saying, review a white paper or two, and pinpoint the industry leaders. Trust is established online. That's where opinions are shared, biases are formed, and rapport is established through videos, podcasts, webinars, forums, and Facebook groups.

Social listening is the process of monitoring digital conversations to understand what clients are saying about a brand and industry online. It is a critical component of the marketing plan because the results, accuracy, and timeliness that social listening affords are invaluable.

Social media alone has become a critical avenue for client complaints and other chatter. It is much easier for someone to fire off a fifty-word Twitter rant on the bus ride home than it is to sit on the phone with client service for hours to lodge a complaint. Paying attention to what people are saying—bad or good—is an excellent opportunity for companies to get ahead of the problem and prevent it from spiraling into a massive issue. Also, by listening to what people ask for online, marketing is able to better understand where the needs are.

To pique the interest of potential clients online, the marketing message needs to be strong and compelling enough to stand out. It also needs to be consistent. Even if you have a fantastic new product and a wonderful sales team, success cannot be counted on without a powerful story to attract people. They will still narrow down the companies they want to speak to, but if you're not delivering the content, you're not even at the negotiating table.

If your marketing efforts are not mobile centric, then you are not serious about client engagement. Virtually everyone has a mobile phone, even the older generations. Pharmacies remind people when to renew their prescriptions via text messages, and doctors and dentists send appointment reminders by text and e-mail. The marketing activity that surrounds client engagement is not restricted to a specific demographic; it is truly universal and therefore cannot be overlooked.

The Australian government uses mobile and Internet technology almost exclusively. Even those who are resistant to computers are forced to learn how to use them if they want access to their tax information and other official paperwork in a timely manner. In 2016, Australia conducted the census online for the first time. Although there were huge issues, the direction was clear.

Clients are attracted to thorough and efficient access to information. The purpose of marketing is to *inform* clients' decisions through education. Then, sales people come in to *enable* that decision. Further, effective marketing begins as simply being aware of how people spend their time, and more specifically, how they research information about your product or service.

Look to your own data to find the kind of targeted information that should be used to drive marketing decisions and planning. Google Analytics is a powerful tool for capturing user behavior and measuring the effectiveness of your website, and it's completely free. Google provides users with an analytical code to cut and paste into their websites that tracks traffic. The level of detail you can learn about visitors to your site is staggering:

- Through what channels are clients coming to your website? How did they hear about you?
- What content promoted them to visit your site? Was it a Facebook ad, a recent webinar, or an e-mail campaign?
- How long did they stay on the site?
- Where did they click?
- Which buttons are being ignored?
- At what point did they leave?

This data is valuable because it allows you to adjust your content and design for enhanced engagement. You can track precisely which marketing behaviors were responsible for lead generation. The reporting functionality occurs in real time, so you know your data is current and accurate.

A TRUE STORY

I was doing some consulting work with a law firm. By monitoring the analytics, I was able to predict an incoming phone call from a client as well as pinpoint the specific legal advice he would inquire about. Within an hour, the phone rang and it was our man, calling to ask about exactly the topic he had hovered on for the past thirty minutes.

The partners were astounded. It wasn't magic though; it was data!

After a few weeks of working with the firm, I was able to get a clear sense of what users were looking for. That knowledge helped to inform the marketing strategy. We knew what topics we needed to provide more resources for, which led to more articles, white papers, and podcasts. At that point, the traffic to the site and the phone calls to the firm became self-perpetuating. We became the go-to resource for a relevant issue, which generated more interest, which led to more clients.

If someone clicked on a certain article, they were automatically sent a follow-up article a few days later with an e-mail that said, "We noticed you were interested in X and thought you might find Y informative as well." The marketing automation worked beautifully.

Once we engaged in a few weeks of follow-up with a prospect, that person then received a personalized e-mail from the principle of the firm that said, "I hope you found the articles and reports we've been sending to you helpful. Please do not hesitate to let me know if you need any further assistance. I am the firm's expert in X area of the law, and I am happy to discuss your questions in greater detail."

More often than not, the person replied to the principle's e-mail and outlined all of their issues—sometimes even their life story—and became a client. We landed on a winning formula. Marketing automation helps your company stay top of mind and in front of potential clients.

THE DATA WILL SET YOU FREE

The level of detailed information available to marketers is only increasing with the more time people spend online. There are numerous tools and platforms that bring data, marketing, and automation together.

ONE YEAR EQUALS SEVEN YEARS

Half the money I spend on advertising is wasted; the trouble is I don't know which half.

—JOHN WANAMAKER

Half the time you spend discussing what advertising will work is wasted; the trouble is you haven't tested which half.

—STEVE DE MAMIEL

In the old days, sales and marketing teams would meet and discuss the marketing plan for the coming year. There would be lots of discussion about what the message would be, what channels would be used, and how the message would be delivered. The more senior members of the team shaped the outcome of the debates, while considering the biases and experience of the others in the room.

The marketing plan created was based on a pretty good guess at what would work. The team would go off and set plans in place and spend all the money as allocated until the end of the annual campaign. The results would be reviewed at the end of the year, and there would be a realization that some campaigns just didn't work. Those that didn't would be dropped for the following year, and those that worked would be continued—and so the cycle repeated.

Today, the marketing cycle is at least seven times faster as a result of A/B testing. Teams can learn as much about how effective their efforts are in one year as they did in seven. Results can be measured hourly, weekly, monthly, or by any time period you choose, making marketing far more dynamic and responsive. The marketing team can put a program in place and watch it succeed or fail in very short intervals with modest amounts of spending.

There is simply no excuse for sitting around debating what might work and spending large sums of money on campaigns that have mixed results. Instead, all the ideas need to be thrown on the table, and the campaigns built and tested. Let the clients say which one worked. Monitor them and see what is working with a modest proportion of the budget before fully committing.

WHAT IS A/B TESTING?

As the phrase suggests, it is a comparison of the different versions of a campaign to see which performs the best. There may be minor differences in the two campaigns, such as channel, message, or what's being offered. They can run for a short period, and the results are monitored. Based on an agreed metric to determine effectiveness, the most successful campaign is continued with the balance of the marketing time and budget.

The marketing cycle for such testing and shifting of the message can be brief enough that a marketer can use it for short events. For example, I have seen a supplier run and test various campaigns for a two-day event. The marketing cycle was monitored by the hour and the campaign was tweaked until the phone started ringing and the orders started pouring through the website.

1 YEAR = 7 ~~DOG~~ MARKETING YEARS

The sales and marketing teams need to move at least seven times faster than they did five years ago to keep up. There is no longer a need to wait to see the success of a campaign—just get it out there, monitor it hourly or daily, and quickly kill off the money wasters. A year is a very long time in a marketing plan. It needs to be monitored and adjusted constantly, and the benefits of spending money where it does the most good will be immediately felt.

ANALYTICS AND ALERTS

Analytics combined with marketing automation allows you to track the full life cycle of prospects. Because their details have been captured just by visiting your website, you can see which e-mails they opened and which ones they didn't. You know what headlines appealed to them and where they clicked. You know their interests and behaviors, and you have the opportunity to communicate with them directly.

Ten years ago, companies spent upwards of $50,000 on their websites. Then, they'd sit there and wait. There was no system to measure the site's effectiveness, let alone in real time. I frequently hear people say they don't use analytics because they don't get a lot of traffic to their website. If that's the case, the problem is with your site. If you're not effectively executing on the single most important foundation for your marketing efforts, you're missing a huge opportunity to understand your clients.

Google Alerts scans every media outlet possible to track whatever search terms you set up. You'll know immediately when your company has been mentioned and in what context. Analytics, and Google Alerts specifically, allow you to monitor what is going on with your business and what people are saying about you. This feeds into the importance of social listening, which we touched on earlier.

In the old days, companies hired public relations firms on retainer to monitor media mentions, and each week, they received a summary of where the company had been covered. They also ran expensive focus groups or conducted client surveys—activities that involved a long lag time.

Now, we have instant access across multiple channels, and we're able to patch together patterns. These themes can be incredibly useful to identify client problems or product benefits, and they're a great way to drive innovation and product development. You can very easily see what's on people's minds, and it's fast, free market research. The information allows companies to tweak their messaging so it is immediately relevant for their clients.

LOOK WHO'S TALKING

For large marketing departments, social listening helps to identify influencers and advocates by their source. Those key opinions could come from individuals, brands, media outlets, bloggers, or certain geographical locations. Knowing who and where your fans or detractors are is critical for connecting with them.

- Where are people looking for information?
- Who is generating content about you?
- Where is the content coming from?

- Are others engaging with it, and if yes, how so?
- What are they saying?
- What is the nature of the comments?
- Is the content being shared?

If someone wanted to buy a high-end road-racing bike and was looking for guidance, where would he turn? Before he steps foot in a bike shop, he'll look at online racing forums and Facebook groups to see where others are discussing the options.

Aside from social listening, there are a variety of offline channels that marketing departments need to stay on top of. For example, does your particular industry have associations affiliated with it? Does the industry association publish material on a regular basis? If so, what kind of news do they cover? What type of message do they deliver to the target client base? If you commit the time and energy to participate in industry associations, you have the opportunity to influence the message and reach the clients directly. That type of access can be tremendously powerful.

The IT sector's associations are influential organizations on their own. Outlets such as Forrester and Garner are the go-to resources for identifying key players in the field and getting to know your competition. They are well known for their independent, unbiased, and timely commentary on industry trends and emerging markets.

MOBILE MARKETING 101

Regardless of where and how you listen to your clients, it is imperative to reach the mobile and digital audience. To do so, your website design must be mobile friendly. This means that the content must be easy to read and use on a phone. Use goes beyond simple navigation. For example, capturing client details, filling in forms, or making purchases must be just as easy on the phone as it is on the desktop. Otherwise, you are a making an active choice to disengage with more than 50 percent of your website traffic.

Specifically, keep the user experience top of mind both from a content perspective as well as in the development platform you choose. Don't blindside visitors with an abundance of information or ask them to download data-sucking pdf files. Load time must be very fast. Google has publicly stated that it favors websites with accelerated pages. Keep the limitations of the smaller screen in mind, because when it comes to website design, one size does not fit all.

If you have a landing page for lead capture, make sure visitors don't need to fill out multiple fields. In most cases, a name and e-mail will suffice in the first instance. Further information can be gathered in later interactions as trust is built. Does SMS (short message service) or texting have a place in your marketing program? Many businesses use SMS for appointment reminders, especially with older generations. More frequently, we're seeing marketing messages that say, "If interested, text XYZ," or "For more information, text the word 'more' to XYZ." This message serves the same purpose as "Visit our website at XYZ.com" but it drives people toward a slightly different action.

Messaging can also be triggered based on one's geographical location. If the Wi-Fi is enabled on your cell phone, retailers inside of shopping malls can track your location and text you special, time-stamped offers or coupons. Highly effective as an automated call-to-action prompt, messaging is filtering into mainstream marketing practices with higher frequency.

Many businesses immediately think about apps when they think about mobile marketing. Apps are cool, they're relatively inexpensive to create, and they can be great for branding, but they're not right for every business. In fact, unless you have an above-average transaction rate or are providing live, up-to-the-minute information, apps can be a distraction from your marketing message.

In many cases it is more effective to be listed on someone else's app than to create your own. For example, many restaurants in the United States have partnerships with OpenTable to manage reservations. It's simpler and easier for both the restaurant and the client to go to one place to manage their reservations. Uber is another great example. The app aggregates available drivers in a few simple clicks, rather than the client having to call around to schedule a cab.

Another website feature to consider is live chat. Chat is almost compulsory for large businesses, and it's becoming more so for smaller businesses. If the decision process involves multiple variables, or there are elements of the purchase a client may see as risky, chat is an important support mechanism.

Keeping up with tech trends can easily be a full-time job. Given how married society is to mobile, marketing departments the world over need to rethink their strategies and find people where they are, which is hunkered down over their phones, just like Sam was when he got a bone.

BEST IN SHOW: MASTERING YOUR DIGITAL MARKETING PLATFORM

1. Know the typical searches for your industry.

- ♛ What are people searching for online?

- ♛ Where are they searching?

- ♛ How can you incorporate that information on your mobile and desktop platforms?

2. Measure your success.

- ♛ How are people behaving when they visit your site?

- ♛ What pages are they spending time on?

- ♛ What is their flow through the website?

- ♛ Where are they leaving the website? Can you test why they are leaving?

3. Engage with your audience.

- ♛ Are you dealing with social media commentary about your business or industry?

- ♛ Make yourself an integral part of the conversation, which is a mark of business maturity.

- ♛ Digitally sophisticated companies have moved from pushing content out to engaging in and being a part of the online conversation.

CHAPTER 2

POODLES BITE TOO

When I worked at the vineyard in the cellar sales, there was a beautiful shaft of light that came through the doorway in the mornings. In the afternoons, when the sun had passed overhead, the same spot was quite cool. Sam favored this spot when it was sunny, as did the winemaker's huge French poodle. The two of them basked in the sunlight and waited for visitors to come by.

I used to watch people as they walked up to the doorway of cellar sales. They stopped and looked at Sam and the poodle lying there blocking their path. The visitors hesitated before entering and wondered which dog was the safest to step over to get inside. Unsurprisingly, most people chose to step over the poodle, assuming that because he was so fluffy and French looking, he was the least aggressive. Sam was a German shepherd cross, which has a reputation for being a fierce and aggressive guard dog. To my great amusement, it was always the poodle that was startled by the visitors and jumped quickly with a snap of his teeth.

Poodles have a reputation for being friendly and docile. The people who visited the vineyard assumed, incorrectly as it turned out, that this one was no different. Well, they were in for a surprise when Sam, the mongrel mutt, dozed lazily in the sun with barely an eye open, as the poodle tried to remove their pant leg.

WHAT IS YOUR CLIENT'S INTENT?

The assumptions people made about the poodle remind me of the assumptions many businesses make about their target market. Most organizations build their market segments or buying personas based on assumptions about their clients. Then, they drive their marketing messages and activities to match their assumptions, which are often based on demographics and psychographics: gender, age, location, annual income, or personality type.

A few decades ago, that information was all we had access to. We had to develop a set of fixed assumptions, or make an educated guess, about what the client looked like because we had to formulate a message. Today, marketing initiatives need to focus on the client's *intent*, and the message should be crafted accordingly.

The old-school marketer was dependent on his or her gut feelings, biases, experiences, and small data sets to create marketing personas. Artificial intelligence and data are shifting the focus from client segmentation and personas to client intent. As these new tools gain market acceptance and find their way into more marketing and sales applications, the old personas are no longer relevant. Marketing now has the tools to be more predictive.

A lot of companies moved away from personas and demographics by accident. By simply nurturing leads based on content consumed and online engagement, marketers are acting on the customer intent, rather than their profiles of the customer. For example, once a purchase is made, a client might start to look for complimentary add-ons. If someone bought a bike, she might also be in the market for lights, bags, and a helmet. More specifically, the add-ons she might need for a road bike are different than the add-ons she might need for a racing bike.

The point is that client intent should drive sales and marketing planning. It starts with lead nurturing and continues past the first purchase. The goal is to create a customer for life and bring that individual into the company's community, where he will become an advocate for the brand.

To identify clients' intent, we need to look closely at what type of information clients search for. What topics are they interested in? What white papers do they download? What buttons do they click on certain websites? What online groups do they engage with? These actions indicate intentions, which is where marketing efforts should be directed.

WHO ARE YOUR CLIENTS AND WHAT DO THEY NEED?

I'll give you an example of how making assumptions about your client base can misfire. I was recently working with a self-storage facility. They assumed that their typical client was a single, forty-five-year-old female, who lived in a townhouse in an inner-city suburb. In turn, they crafted a female-centric marketing message that promoted smaller facilities to accommodate apartment overflow.

When they delved a little deeper into who their clients actually were, they discovered that a variety of factors led their female-based clientele to rent storage space. Often it was because a parent had moved into a retirement facility or died, or they were going through a divorce. If the marketing message was more aligned with their clients' true needs, they would have experienced higher occupancy rates at the facility. It might have been more effective to craft a message that said, "Mrs. Smith, you've got enough on your plate. If you don't have enough storage space, we've got a solution!"

The storage facility also catered to a number of contractors who had extra tools and building supplies. They needed a place for the overflow of items that their wives wouldn't let them keep at home or for things they didn't use every day. Tools and supplies are expensive, so this clientele was primarily concerned with the security of the facility.

Due to early morning appointments, they also wanted twenty-four-hour access.

Because the facility was solely focused on their client base of single, forty-five-year-old females living in townhouses, the contractors were excluded entirely from the marketing message. They would have been able to capture a nice niche market segment had they better marketed the safety and convenience of the facility.

The storage facility had correctly identified *who* some of their clients were, but they failed to identify *why* the clients needed help. They ignored their primary market's "pain," while simultaneously disregarding the secondary client segment altogether. If they had focused on the issues that triggered the demand for their services, they would have enjoyed greater success. Who you market to and what message you deliver are two different things, and you cannot market on assumptions alone.

DUMP THE DEMOGRAPHICS

Examining clients through a segmented, demographic lens is limiting and often inaccurate. It is based purely on a set of assumptions and biases about people.

I'll give you another example. My son is eleven years old, and he is fascinated by old-time amateur radio (also known as ham radio). The technology on these radios has come a long way since they were first invented in the 1940s, but the basic premise is the same. He became interested in them because we do a lot of camping, and I have a high-frequency radio in our four-wheel drive because of the distances we cover.

From Melbourne, my son talks to people all over the world. A license is required to operate ham radios, and they have quite a cult following. In fact, my son is part of a ham radio enthusiast's club; he is the only one in the room under the age of sixty-five. Ham radio marketers don't take the younger generation into consideration at all. They assume the vast majority of their client base are men over the age of fifty-five, and the sales message is delivered accordingly with limited online marketing.

Interestingly, this group of ham radio enthusiasts is very active online, because they love to talk about equipment and share information. My son spends every available cent on his ham radio equipment. From a marketing standpoint, he is a red-hot client, as are all the middle-aged men he communicates with at the club and online. Just like the storage facility, the CB radio marketers have overlooked their client's intent. They focused instead on assumptions and biases of who their clients are, thereby missing out on their most active and avid fan base. The fact is, there is no such thing as a "typical" client base anymore.

SAMUEL SAYS: MARKETING SHOULD BE DRIVEN BY CLIENT INTENT.

What intentional actions do your clients make during the buying process to resolve an issue or gain a benefit? Those actions offer opportunities for engagement and lead generation. Also, what stage of intent is the client in? How close are they to engaging with a salesperson and making a buying decision?

TRIGGERING CLIENT INTENT

When clients are on the verge of tackling the issue, marketers can trigger their intent by showing them the future state. For example, if someone exhibits strong early signs of buying a new road-racing bicycle, marketing can tailor the message to include the bike's performance ratings or testimonials from current owners.

Companies are responsible for showing their clients the path to a solution for their problems. Present a call to action, such as: "Enter our drawing to win tickets to the annual road race." Attending an event allows clients an opportunity to see the bike in action—how well it handles hills, corners, distances, and all of its other features.

If client intent is already obvious, details will help clients make a buying decision. They've already done their research, and they're close to engaging with a salesperson. Relevant messaging can tip the sale, such as: "Test-ride the lightest road-racing bike in its class," or "The world's best riders report that this bike allows them to cover more kilometers in comfort." The key is to demonstrate what the client's situation will look like after the issue has been resolved.

Once client intent has been identified, it also needs to be tracked and measured. Google Analytics, again, will be a useful tool in this endeavor. Facebook also captures specific search criteria and other valuable marketing data such as marital status, geographic location, interests, and likes. You want to know how and where people hear about your company, which helps tailor the specificity of your message.

MARKETING = EDUCATION AND INFLUENCE

Educating the client is the realm of marketing, whereas selling is the process of decision enablement. There needs to be a clear line of demarcation in this regard. If someone requires further information, she needs to be directed to marketing. More often than not, clients form their own opinions through groups online anyway. Salespeople have very little chance of unraveling preconceived notions. They're not likely to be believed or capable of overturning twenty other reviews. Plus, it's not the best use of their time to attempt to do so.

The best way to get ahead of the story is to control it through understanding intent and triggering it. For example, if someone is getting ready to sell her house, the first thing she does is contact a real-estate agent. The agent visits the home and evaluates how to get the best price for it. In many instances, the agent tells the owner, "The house is more likely to sell if you get rid of some of the clutter. Have you considered putting 50 percent of your belongings in storage so the house appears more spacious?" The homeowner is not a storage facility client yet, but the real-estate agent has triggered the intent. Bingo.

At this point, the homeowner transitions into the research gathering with the intention of figuring out how much storage they need and how much it will cost. An initial online search for the basic questions triggers a deeper dive: Does the client need temperature control, twenty-four-hour access, or security features?

While the client is gathering information, marketing is responsible for assessing the homeowner's needs, educating her on the options available, and painting the picture. "From our experience, a person with a three-bedroom house requires X amount of storage. We can help you think through your specific needs and come up with a solution for your scenario."

The self-storage facility should have a defined follow-up process and determine at which point the client needs further information or a phone call. Often the process unfolds on a case-by-case basis. If the client has already used self-storage, she likely has a good idea of what she needs and doesn't require further education. She can engage with a sales representative sooner than someone who is new to the service.

RELATIONSHIP BUILDING

Companies need to be wary of falling into a transactional relationship trap with their clients. This can occur when companies "jump the gun" on sales, or worse, focus exclusively on making the sale. The integration of marketing and sales is a relatively new science. Marketers are accustomed to qualifying a lead, handing it over to sales, and then washing their hands of it. They have successfully completed the first phase of their efforts, but it needn't end there.

To enhance the company's relationship with the client, sales and marketing activities must be integrated. Marketing needs to be involved with the client long before they show up at the door, and in many cases, they need to remain involved throughout the client life cycle.

For example, the purchase of a new road-racing bike is not the end of the relationship with that client. On the contrary, the purchase is the first step in what could and should be a long-term relationship. What new accessories or enhancements are available for that bike? Do you offer any deals on service? The marketing department needs to stay attuned to the client's journey to find new opportunities.

If, on the other hand, the client is not ready to buy a new road-racing bike, or there are factors outside of his control, no amount of prodding from sales is going to make a difference. At that point, the best course of action is to determine how to remain engaged with the client, without being pushy, through ongoing education. Send the client relevant, valuable information every few weeks to stay connected. Determine what will enhance the client experience by letting him know about related products or services. Amazon, Apple, and Netflix do this by making suggestions based on the client's unique interests. For example, "Because you watched *Braveheart*, you might enjoy *Last of the Mohicans*."

CREATING COMMUNITY

Once a sale has been made, stage two of marketing maturity is keeping the client. By participating in the lifetime value of the client, marketing can help to rebuild the pipeline with future sales as the client becomes a more engaged buyer. Lululemon has been successful in building a loyal community behind the brand by keeping their clients involved long after a sale. When someone buys an item of clothing from one of their stores, they're then invited to participate in yoga classes and other events in the area. Lululemon is not just looking at what people buy; they're looking at how people are using their apparel. As a result, their clients are extremely connected to the brand and deeply loyal.

Harley-Davidson is also well known for keeping their loyal clients engaged. In fact, they added a popular apparel brand on top of their motorcycles. Harley clients wear a certain type of clothing, so who better to create that clothing than Harley? When someone buys a new bike and is loyal to the brand, they're likely also to buy the appropriate apparel for riding. The brand extension was a natural marketing opportunity for the organization, and a highly profitable one. Harley has clearly defined their community culture.

The most successful companies are those that understand the life cycle of their clients. They engage with their clients at each stage to the degree that they are able to create a new community. Marketing and sales work in tandem as the client goes through the initial buying process and beyond. They are in touch with their client's intent, or what the client is trying to move toward or away from.

Don't fall into the assumption trap, as the visitors to the vineyard cellars did when they saw Sam and the French poodle dozing in the doorway. Approach your clients with eyes wide open, so you can see them without bias brought about by market segmentation. Look only at the demonstrated actions, or as I call it, the client intent. Leave the preconceived notions behind to have real interactions, and provide them with long-lasting value.

BEST IN SHOW: UNDERSTANDING AND TRIGGERING CLIENT INTENT

1. Identify what is triggering your clients' actions.

- 🏆 Gain an understanding of what happens both before and after your clients make a purchase.

- 🏆 What things need to happen before they buy something and what things need to happen after? These are good indications of intention.

2. What are your clients' stages of intent?

- 🏆 Does your marketing strategy recognize and align with those stages?

- 🏆 Review your current sales and marketing. Is any of it influenced by bias or preconceptions rather than data and/or client intent?

3. Engage with potential clients.

- 🏆 Who are the influencers and advocates in your industry?

- 🏆 How and where are you engaging with them?

4. Make sure your clients remain with you.

- 🏆 How do your clients receive further information, after their purchase?

- 🏆 Are you providing value and keeping them engaged?

5. Reduce the risk for your clients.

- 🏆 This needs to be done through vehicles such as ratings systems, publishing timelines, or illuminating processing times.

6. Create a client community.

- 🏆 Does your client base belong to an existing community? If so, what can you do to engage, influence, and provide thought leadership within that community?

- 🏆 Is there an opportunity for you to build an online or offline community?

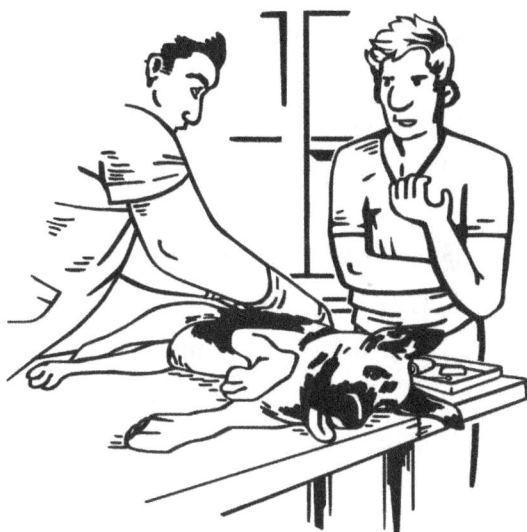

CHAPTER 3

GOING TO THE VET

Being the crazy, retrieving mutt that he was, Sam always had to have something to chase or chew on. If his slobbery ball was taken away from him—as it often was—he went in search of a stick or a rock to gnaw. We never knew what it was he had in his mouth because he guarded it so protectively.

Unsurprisingly, one day he accidentally swallowed a mystery object and had to be taken to the vet. Sam had a habit of using rocks he found in the vineyard if his slobbery ball was confiscated, which happened often. People got sick of a disgusting ball being pushed at them to throw. I assumed he got a little overzealous and ingested one while on the run, but the vet wasn't so sure.

Rather than dive straight in and treat Sam for an ingested rock, instead, he asked me a series of questions. He asked about Sam's overall health, what he had been doing just before the incident, and how his behavior in general seemed. From there, the vet proceeded to prod and poke and check things out. He did a round of tests, and once he had determined what the problem was, he went on to treat it.

Systematically, the vet followed a process of prognosis and then diagnosis. I felt comfortable that the vet had explored all the options and given Sam a thorough examination. He didn't jump to conclusions, as I had, or rush into any assumptions.

THE ASSUMPTION TRAP

In a sales scenario, often the client superficially names his or her problem. A lot of salespeople fall into the trap of immediately rushing in to offer a solution. They'll tell the client they've seen the problem many times before and they know exactly how to handle it. They'll try to demonstrate that they are more than capable of coping with the problem and making it go away.

This common response raises a few issues. When the salesperson dives straight into talking about solutions, she has missed out on the opportunity to uncover the client's real issues. Usually, this scenario unfolds because the salesperson is *anticipating* what the client is going to say, rather than *listening* to what he is saying. She's eager to show the client what she can do, but they she winds up pre-empting him. This can cause people to get a little defensive or feel put off. Everyone wants to finish his thought when he is speaking and feel as if he has been heard.

It's not advised for the salesperson to guess, tell, or even accept what the client says straight out of the gate. The relationship is too new, and the walls of resistance are still very much intact. The client will likely provide only a superficial description and incomplete list of the issues. This is exactly why we cannot make sales based on assumptions or blindly accept what the client says he needs.

HARD LESSON LEARNED

When I first moved to Sydney from Perth (Sam came too, ending his winery career), I was chasing business with large insurance and banking clients. I was often competing with large global-system integrators who paid little to no attention to my company as a competitor. Although we had great ideas, people, and technology, we lacked the comfort that came with a big consulting firm.

One day, I was presenting to one of Australia's largest banks. I was introduced by one of the largest health insurers, so I was off to a good start with solid credibility and a reference point.

The burning issue in the back of my mind was that I knew IBM had a long-established relationship with this bank account. How was I going to get the bank to take a risk on my company's ability to execute? The old cliché "Nobody got sacked by choosing IBM" was playing in the back of my mind. After all, I was dealing with conservative bankers.

Despite my fears, the presentation went well and things were looking good. My demo made us look like we had already built the solution the bank wanted. We pulled out all the stops to minimize the bank's risk in working with us.

Then finally, the dreaded questions came. They asked: How many people do you have? How many offices do you have? Who are some of your largest clients? What do you do for them?

Well, I went into overdrive. My two-person service office suddenly sounded like a technology hot spot, swarming with experts. Sydney's main banks, insurers, and telcos were lining up outside the door.

When I finally paused for a breath of air, the response was, "Oh, it sounds like you're very busy!" "Oh yes," I said, emphasizing how big and important our clients were and how much work we had on the table with them all.

Before I had a chance to go further, I was interrupted and told, "That's a shame you are so swamped. We are looking for someone who can be very focused on our account. We will be a major contributor to their revenue, and we want to make sure we can get the support we've been lacking for this business unit. In fact, we heard that one of the SIs is interested in buying your business. We just recently established a venture capital fund and thought adding you as a vendor had a number of advantages. Why don't you get on top of your workload and come back and talk to us?"

I completely blew it! I assumed I knew what the real question was and went into overdrive defending an issue that didn't exist. If I had just kept quiet, we would have won the business. To make matters worse, I took a fair bit of artistic license in describing our local resource base. The bank had already looked into that to see if it fitted the mandate for their venture capital fund.

By jumping straight into a prognosis before a diagnosis, I had blown up a huge potential sale. I wasn't looking forward to the conversation with the owner of the business back in Perth that afternoon! I could have asked any number of questions to get to the real issue. Instead, I messed the whole thing up by jumping to a conclusion and assuming I knew what the real issue was.

GRANDDAD IS STRICT

These painful experiences of making assumptions could happen to anyone. In fact, it just happened to my own daughter who was trying to build the case about why she needs a mobile phone. I've been resistant to letting her have one for some time now, and she is growing rather desperate.

I noticed that my daughter started being extra helpful around the house and unusually sweet. She was clearly going out of her way to demonstrate exemplary behavior and manners. I know pretty well when I'm being buttered up, and I let her carry on, amused at the lengths she was going to make a favorable impression on her mother and me.

After dinner one night, I was enjoying my coffee on the couch, and my daughter slid up next to me. My internal alarm bells were blowing off the hinges. Without any preamble, she said, "May I please get a mobile phone?" Before I had a chance to answer, she rattled off a string of examples of times when she had needed a phone but had not one. In every single one of her stories, either I had been inconvenienced or she had been in some sort of danger. There was that time when she got lost at the shopping mall and the time she couldn't find a ride home after basketball practice. There was that time I had to leave an important appointment to go collect her from school at the last minute.

Skillfully, my daughter talked through all of my possible objections. Her argument was well structured. I started to think I was in trouble. She had made an excellent case, and I couldn't come up with a single reason to refuse her. She had built her case with the benefits I would receive at the very center. She outlined all the ways that I would be better off if she had a phone.

Just as I was about to concede defeat, she made a fatal error. In a raised and excited voice, thinking she had it in the bag, she punctuated her carefully crafted case by saying, "And come on, Dad, how old were *you* when Granddad let you have your first mobile?" I stopped to think about it and said, "I was twenty-two." A look of shock came over my nine-year-old's face. She looked over at her mum to see if this was true. Her mother nodded in ascent. My daughter was furious and stormed out of the room. She was last heard saying, "I didn't know Granddad was so strict!"

She had completely overlooked that mobile phones haven't always been around, and they certainly haven't always been a rite of passage for a nine-year-old. She assumed she had the argument on lockdown, but she didn't have all the facts. If she had not made the assumption that I grew up with mobile phones too, she would have won the argument. It was sad to see, but I bought myself some time before having to make the commitment to buy her a phone.

KEEP DIGGING FOR HARD EVIDENCE

🐾 Keep digging for evidence that the solution has a value.

🐾 Without hard evidence, the solution has no value.

🐾 The evidence may be either *HARD* or *SOFT*.

HARD

🐾 You can measure it, now and into the future.

🐾 e.g. "This widget costs $xx.xx to add to the solution."

🐾 e.g. "This step of the process takes xx days to complete."

SOFT

🐾 Gut feel

🐾 Rough Estimate

🐾 e.g. "We think / It should"

🐾 e.g. "I'm not sure"

If the evidence is soft

TO FIND THE BONE

✖ Who has the numbers?

✖ Who owns that process?

✖ How do we confirm that?

Rather than using a script, engage in conversation with your client. Try framing the initial discussion with exploratory questions that get the client to open up: "Thanks for telling me about that issue. What does success look like in your business if we solve that issue? What will you be able to do that you cannot do today? What outcome are you trying to achieve?" When you can dive down into the impact the solution will have and get the other person to describe it for you, you can start to uncover how serious he or she is about investing in the outcome. You're in the process of uncovering hard evidence around some of the symptoms that are causing the client problems.

When I took Sam to the vet, it was the evidence that determined his treatment, not my interpretation of why we were there. Likewise, in sales, the actual measureable or observable evidence needs to drive the final solution for the client.

SOFT AND HARD EVIDENCE

Clients often do what I did in the visit to the vet. They start describing their issues or respond to questions with what is referred to as "soft evidence." Soft evidence is what we presume the case might be. Either we indirectly heard what we thought the case might be or we took an educated guess.

For example, the client might say, "We are looking for a solution to eliminate this manual task from our process. We think we can save money if we automate the process." The obvious questions are likely: How long does it take now? How many people are involved? And what other costs do you incur in the process?

If we were working with an IT manager assigned the task of making a recommendation as to the best solution, he may not know the current process in detail and may well be inclined to say. "I think it takes about five people and roughly five days." This response is soft evidence because it's based on an educated guess. It's an estimate or a gut feeling. It's what the IT manager *thinks* it is, not what he *knows* it is.

Unfortunately, most salespeople are inclined to take that answer and run with it. The IT manager could be off by one day or one person, which is a 20 percent variance for each key cost component! That sort of inaccuracy is critical when developing a business case. Not many businesses would take on the risk and cost of a process change with such loose key criteria.

The salesperson's responsibility is to work with hard evidence. In this example, the hard evidence is exactly how many people and how many days the process takes. Hard evidence can be measured accurately over a defined time period. There is no guessing. It is real evidence that a lawyer or police officer would be happy to work with.

The challenge is how to get the hard evidence if the person you're dealing with only has the soft evidence. The salesperson needs to be alert for clues that indicate the person she is speaking to may not have all the facts. For example, "I *think* it'll take five people and five days" is a clue. The trick is getting in front of the person who has the hard evidence without the IT manager feeling like he's been sidelined. To do that, the salesperson needs to explain the importance of the hard evidence to the business case.

For example: "Given that you need to establish the business case for this project, would it make sense that we talk to the head of operations? An exact number will help us to establish the baseline costs."

Identify why you need the hard evidence. Not only will it help you to get the correct information, but it gets you in front of the additional stakeholders who are sitting around the table making the decision (see chapter 4).

SAMUEL SAYS: DIAGNOSIS SHOULD ALWAYS PRECEDE PROGNOSIS.

Clients also make assumptions. Be alert to opportunities to elaborate on an issue or correct the client if it becomes apparent that she thinks she already knows everything there is to know about your product or service. For example, a client may walk into a furniture store and tell the salesperson she is interested in buying a red leather couch. The salesperson might say in response, "I don't have red leather, but I have black and I have brown." At that point, the conversation might stall out, but if the salesperson explores exactly what the client is looking for a bit further, he may well likely uncover the client's true driver.

Many times clients have preconceived notions about what they want. Maybe the client in the furniture shop saw a photo of a red leather couch and it stuck in her mind. Somewhere, an opinion was formed, even though it may not represent what the client actually wants. Perhaps the client saw a red leather couch, but it also happened to be a three-seater, convertible sofa bed.

After a little digging, the salesperson can drill down to what the client is really looking for, which is not actually a red leather couch. She really wants a three-seater convertible sofa bed, but the one she saw just happened to be red leather. Salespeople need to be keen to this sort of preconception because the client's true needs often require investigating before they are identified.

If there is a complex, business-to-business sale on the table, the tendency for the client to lob soft issues at the salesperson usually increases. For example, if an IT manager is shopping around for automation software, he may say that he wants a system that will shave two days off of the process. The salesperson will automatically hear "speed." Speed may very well be part of what the client is looking for, but there's always more to it.

The IT manager might be making assumptions about what his operations manager wants out of the software. He also might assume a process that requires ten people can be reduced to five people, which will, therefore, impact internal staffing needs. The point is that assumptions of any sort need to be taken out of the mix to get to the heart of the matter, just as I experienced with the Australian bank.

Once the salesperson has gone through the proper diagnosis, he or she can get closer to what the real solution will be. That kind of valuable information is what leads to an opportunity to make a sale. If we just accept what the client tells us, the sale could easily run off the road, as it almost did at the furniture store. We have to test both our own and the client's assumptions before we can get closer to resolution.

How do we avoid making assumptions in the sales process? To start, salespeople need to change their reflex reaction. Instead of simply agreeing to deliver a solution, the reflex should be to understand the problem, when the client would like it resolved by, and what's brought it to a head now. The full context of the problem needs to be examined because nothing happens in isolation.

If you are speaking to someone from a large organization, there will be multiple stakeholders involved in the decision-making process. It's important to understand who is involved and how they will be affected. If the person you are speaking to doesn't have the hard evidence, you need to determine who does and propose a meeting with that person.

An appropriate way to handle this is to say, "Clearly this decision is an important one for your business. Would it make sense for us to meet with your operations manager to confirm the benefits our product can provide for your particular issue?" You are helping to build the business case by enlisting the approval of the person who has the hard evidence. These deeper conversations save everyone from charging down a fruitless path.

If someone wants to implement software that reduces the time it takes to do a job by half and frees up five people from doing a task, those five people are the hard evidence. Very few organizations are going to make a large IT investment based on a vague notion of time saved. Both the salesperson and the client need to identify the return on investment. The solution only earns value when a problem is solved or a benefit is delivered.

NO HARD EVIDENCE?

What if there is no hard evidence? It's not unusual that the client will not or cannot move beyond general reasons around why they want to make the investment. The client indicates they want to move ahead, yet the evidence is not there to support the business case or the expenditure. In this case, we are not looking at a return on investment; we are simply looking at a cost. Maybe the client is saying, "Don't worry about the actual numbers or time; we know we need to do this."

Alternatively, they might be saying something that is unrelated to the business case, such as "It's an improvement we need to make," or "It's an issue we need to solve." They might not be prepared to provide introductions to those who have the hard evidence or even to get your list of questions answered by those who have the answers.

The vet wouldn't proceed with a treatment without the evidence. Similarly, sales professionals need to take a hard look at the situation to decide whether they can proceed with a solution.

There are a few options at this critical point. The key is to remember that you are still qualifying the opportunity. Does the client have the time, the resources, and the need? If you cannot find the evidence to prove the need, you need to make a few decisions about how to spend your time.

Although the client contact may be dismissive, you need to have the conversation with the client. The tendency for the salesperson is to charge on regardless. You're hearing a very strong message from the client that this project is going ahead. Having made this mistake myself on more than one occasion, I've learned to really push the point with the client.

On many occasions, I've seen a government department go through a formal tender process. It involved detailed tender preparation, vendor briefings, facility tours, and onsite demonstrations. It even included short-listing vendors. Yet when the recommendation was made to proceed, the project was canceled.

Throughout the process, I knew the business case wasn't there. I knew the investment to implement the solution seemed excessive for the benefit it would deliver. The department insisted that there were side benefits, but none of them were tangible or articulated. No one could or would provide hard evidence of the side benefits.

Despite the alarm bells, I pressed on. I submitted the tender, attended all the briefings, made the demonstrations, flew technical people around the country to assist, but it was all to no avail. In sales, we often experience the disappointment of losing a sale to a competitor. Somehow, it's worse to lose the sale due to the client's inaction. It's easy to blame it on the client, but usually the warning bells were ringing from the outset. It just took client's senior management to make the call.

I hate to admit it, but I've made this kind of mistake more than once. Now, I'm far more protective of my time and well aware that sometimes the client may not have the experience or the skill to see the necessity of the business case. The client contact may have an operational role and see that the overall improvement makes sense, or that their competition is using it, or that they are one of the last to adopt the new technology. Without the hard evidence, the opportunity is not going to move ahead.

THE HARD CONVERSATION

What do you do if you find yourself in a situation where the alarm bells are going off? You have an enthusiastic client who says the job will proceed, but he is blocking you from getting the hard evidence. He simply will not let you near those who have the evidence, or he can't see the value in obtaining the evidence to begin with. If this is the case, you need to directly address the issue. Open the conversation by saying, "I have a concern. I'm confused and I think we might have a problem. Can you talk this through with me, please?" Next, try one of the three following approaches to having the hard conversation.

1. Discuss the customer's internal process.

Take a look at the client's project approval process. Is there a business case that needs to be established? What numbers need to feed into it? Spend some time with the client, and make it clear that the questions you are asking also pertain to building the business case. Be sure to link the evidence you are looking for to the client's own approval process. That way, he understands you're on the same team. Your questions will lead to the answers he needs.

For example, "John, I'm concerned that we haven't established the ROI for this project. I understand you need a business case for project approval. You might recall that

I asked to talk to operations to get the numbers around the cost of the current process. Those numbers will help us to establish if my solution is the right fit for what you need. They'll also help you get a start on the business case."

2. Discuss your experience with other similar clients or projects.

Draw on your previous experience about the approach past clients have taken to your proposed solution. Most clients are keen to hear what their competitors or other companies are up to. You don't need to disclose confidential information, but you can outline what you've seen done in the initial project scoping or vendor selection phases. This could be an opportunity to address your concerns about anything that might be missing in the current approach.

For example, "John, I'm confused. We seem to have missed a couple of steps or important pieces of the process. In the past when I worked with XYZ company, they found value in completing a detailed review of the process they wanted to automate. It gave them the benchmark to establish the ROI on the project. I know we've talked briefly about this, and the numbers were not at hand. When I did the project at XYZ, my solution could be benchmarked against the cost of doing it the old way. Do you see any value in that approach? Given what we currently know,

I'm concerned that my solution cannot be benchmarked or that we can't determine an ROI."

3. Finally, if you're desperate, talk about your own need to justify your time on this project and explore other potential internal resources.

A feeling of desperation can kick in when the opportunity hasn't been properly qualified, especially if you're only talking to one person in the organization who sees the opportunity as a priority. There are red flags around time and resourcing for the project. What you need has limited bearing on what the client should do, but you have strong concerns about the client's ability or willingness to move forward. In this case, let the client know that in order for you to get the resources you need to properly develop the solution for the client, you need to show *your manager* the basic business case, ROI, and why you're the best fit.

For example, "John, I think we have a problem. In order to give you a demo unit for a few days, I need to show my boss why this solution makes sense for you. At the moment, I cannot do this, but I have a list of questions I need answered. Can you help me out?"

If the answer is yes, great, you can move on. If you don't think the opportunity is going to proceed and you want to politely withdraw and move on to something else, leave the issue with the client to solve.

AN EXERCISE IN FUTILITY

I was doing some work for a company that sells domain names in Scottsdale, Arizona. Whenever a client bought a domain name, someone from that company called the client and tried to upsell him or her on value-added services: website design, e-mail blasts, blog posts, stock photos, social media management, and anything else that someone with a new website domain name might need.

The company's sale strategy was anchored in two assumptions:

1. The client was prepared to build a website immediately.
2. The client was also ready to launch a full-scale marketing campaign to support the site.

The salesperson got on the phone and launched into a rehearsed speech about the wonderful support services they offered around the product the client already purchased.

Their success rate with this strategy was terrible, and they were frequently hung up on. In the rare case when they could engage the client in a conversation, they learned that some of the people were buying up domain names to prevent the competition from getting to it first. Some of the domains the company sold were a slight variation on or a misspelling of the client's business name. Most of the clients never intended to purchase additional services. A handful of them bought domains in anticipation of a future business idea that they intended to launch six or twelve months down the road. Unfortunately, they did not have the lead-nurturing process in place to keep the client engaged and had to hand it back to sales to revisit at a later date.

As soon as the salespeople ditched the script and listened to the clients, they were able to say, "Sounds great, Mr. Client. Is it alright with you if I call back in six or twelve months when you might actually benefit from our additional marketing services?" Those clients that chose to engage always said, "Sure. Please do." Guessing a client's needs is an incredibly inefficient means of going about doing business. There needs to be a proper exploration around what is driving the client.

Only Google gets away with guessing—and finishing your sentences. Any other salespeople who do that are seen as arrogant, ignorant, or both. The salesperson who is genuinely interested in the client's outcome is the one who will get the sale.

ASK POINTED QUESTIONS

Taking a diagnostic approach to the client's problem allows for deeper relationships. It goes a long way toward understanding the business case and building trust and rapport. Most people would be dubious of a doctor who heard one or two symptoms and then immediately wrote a prescription. There is a natural process whereby people want to explain the position they're in and talk about what they are trying to achieve and why. A deal is far more likely to go through if those issues are explored and discussed, and the salesperson has a far greater shot at delivering a solution that actually fits the client's needs.

Just as many dogs recognize certain words or commands, so do your clients. They know a canned speech when they hear one. Break down the barriers that stand between you and clients, and ask them pointed questions. I follow pretty much the same routine when trying to solve a problem. After I've asked clients about the two or three key issues, I'll ask them if there is anything else or if anyone else will be affected.

Once I have a context for the issues on the table, we can drill down into which ones are the most important. Often getting to the heart of the hard evidence issue can take months of conversations, which is part of building the relationship. The goal is to identify and remove the roadblocks.

If you are at the beginning stages of a long sales cycle, you want to understand why the client hasn't addressed the problem in the past. What has prevented the client from moving forward before? What constraints did he or she face? Is there a compliance element? What exactly are all parties looking at? It's worth it for the salesperson to invest the time and help the client understand what needs to be resolved before moving forward. If the problem has existed for some time and the client is ready to move forward, you need to ensure that the previous roadblocks have been removed.

PUT YOURSELF IN THEIR SHOES

Enthusiasm is infectious, so exude it when you communicate with your clients. It will make them want to talk to you and engage. There is a tendency for salespeople to look at their clients as a commodity instead of a person. This is especially true if you've been selling the same solution for some time and have heard the same client stories, which will get you exactly nowhere. Concentrate on the future state that the client can achieve with your product. Be clear on what motivates and excites them, and take notice when the client is visualizing. Build on that energy. I have found that clients are far more forgiving of salespeople who might be nervous presenters or lack some up-to-date information if the salesperson is enthusiastic and genuinely interested in what the client wants to achieve for their business.

A salesperson has to harness the excitement the client shows up with. I remember walking through the vineyard with Sam one beautiful, clear, chilly morning. It was autumn, and the leaves were a full golden color and beginning to fall from the trees. As Sam and I walked, I noticed there was some frost damage on the vines that would require at least a few days of pruning. I was grumbling under my breath about everything I had to do. It would be weeks of work.

I walked by a few vacationers who were marveling at the beautiful weather and the incredible location. They told me how lucky I was to be able to work in such a spot. It occurred to me just how differently people look at what is right in front of them. The vacationers saw the beauty; I saw the work ahead.

I see a similar scenario unfold with salespeople who do the same thing day in and day out. They start to commoditize their own product and see only what's immediately in front of them. They see their widget as faster, better, cheaper, whereas the client is actually looking for a buying experience. The client wants to feel excited about the outcome, as the vacationers did at the vineyard.

For example, if someone is in the market for a convertible, she is imagining long drives through the countryside. She's thinking about the wind in her hair and the sunshine on her head as she drives down the Pacific Coast Highway. The salesperson, on the other hand, has extolled the features of the convertible a million times. The excitement of the experience is gone for him. He focuses exclusively on the car's benefits or features, or worse, its price in comparison to other cars, which is not why the client is buying the car.

If the salesperson had engaged with the client about what she wanted to do with the car after purchasing it, he could share in the enthusiasm and share the vision. The salesperson needs to concentrate on the future state that the client can accomplish with the product, rather than on the current state.

That leads to a very different, and far more rewarding, rapport than simply commoditizing one's offerings.

BEST IN SHOW: GOOD SALESPEOPLE LISTEN TO UNDERSTAND; THEY DON'T TALK TO TELL

1. What symptoms do your clients usually present?

2. Check the quality of the evidence.

   🏆 Is it hard or soft?

   🏆 Keep digging until you find the hard evidence.

3. Is there an opportunity for marketing to address the symptoms to attract more prospects?

4. What assumptions about your industry or solution does the client make?

   🏆 Are there assumptions that need to be corrected?

   🏆 Does this provide an opportunity for differentiation or building trust?

5. What are the key questions that you should be asking the client to ensure that you have a complete list of his or her issues or concerns?

CHAPTER 4

WHO WILL FEED
THE DOG?

Picture a stereotypical 1950s family sitting around the dinner table. Dad is just home from work, Mom made a roast, and little Sally and Johnny finished their homework before supper. Everyone's in their places as Dad carves the roast, and the dog sneaks quietly into the room. He knows he's not allowed in the room during mealtimes, but there's always the off chance he'll get lucky and Sally or Johnny will slip him a scrap.

There's some tension in the air. The kids want the dog in the room while they eat, but Dad thinks there should be some better boundaries in this house. He tolerates it, though, because his wife is just sitting there pleasantly trying to keep the peace between everyone so they can enjoy a meal she spent a lot of time preparing.

Because of the group dynamics within the family, there's a bit of give-and-take on everyone's part. The dog is well aware of these dynamics and tries to use them to his benefit. He knows who his allies are and how far to push. He also knows to steer clear of Dad and to behave for Mum. If he lays low and isn't boisterous around the table, she'll advocate for him to stay in the room with the family. To be effective, the dog understands which person is most likely to give him scraps, how long he will have to wait, and what he needs to do to get them.

IDENTIFY THE DECISION MAKERS

Similarly, salespeople must understand how the buying decision is made. In a stereotypical sale scenario, the sales manager instructs his sales team to "go find the decision maker" within an organization. Who signs the checks and has the final say-so? Salespeople have this drummed into them from their first day: anyone beyond the decision maker is a waste of time. Well, this is no longer true, and it's an old-school approach.

The project management and dedicated procurement teams have changed the decision process and in turn changed what the salesperson's approach should be within a business. A successful salesperson who is selling complex solutions into businesses understands that there is one person who leads the decision process but there are a number of people who influence it. Most organizations have elaborate collectives of stakeholders, who all have very different criteria for the solution. There is often a team of decision makers, and no one person should be treated better or differently than the rest.

Most organizations are structured so there's a separation between those who will implement the project and those who will sign off on it. For example, in the IT lead solution described, the technical member of the IT department may be doing the implementation, but operational management may be responsible for the project from a funding perspective. In that case, the operations team is expecting the ROI outlined in the business case.

The important thing is to know who the main players are and what their roles are. The salesperson needs to understand the dynamics of the organization and accept the fact that they are not likely going to get face time with the executive suite. The key is to identify who the key stakeholders are and to determine their individual criteria.

WHO'S AT THE TABLE?

The new approach to sales looks a lot like the old picture of a 1950s family sitting around the table. Everyone has different roles, agendas, and objectives. Everyone is trying to cooperate, but there will always be a degree of underlying tension as a result of the differences. It's important to understand how all the pieces fit together.

The role of the kids at the dinner table might be played by a couple of enthusiastic IT managers who are gunning for a new, cutting-edge system for the office. The operational manager, who is looking more closely at a number of operational issues, might temper their enthusiasm. He plays the role of the dad; he's looking at how the new system might be implemented, what its impact will be, and how they will pay for it. He's looking at where the system falls on the organization's list of priorities and how it fits into their overall strategy.

As a result of organizations becoming larger and having various business functions across floors of a building, or even across counties, selecting a vendor or a solution has become increasingly complex. Large organizations have multiple separate but interdependent departments. Because different departments are responsible for different business objectives or KPIs, they have different funding arrangements. Although the business units, functions, or departments might be physically separated and operate separately, many business initiatives overlap and impact numerous departments. What might be an improvement for one business unit may in fact create work, change, or challenges for another business unit. This results in tension while business units seek some sort of compromise.

Specifically, procurement departments play a larger role than they did in the past. They ensure that processes are fair and that the weighted criteria are considered so that the organization's aims are met. Procurement's involvement in purchasing decisions has served to remove people's biases or personal preferences for certain features or vendors.

Procurement's main goals are to achieve the best price and hold the vendor accountable for deliverables through warranties, service, and support. They are responsible for due diligence to ensure that the vendor is appropriately qualified to follow through. Some view procurement as antisales, but the real objective is to make sure that the transaction between the client and the vendor is in their best interest.

Project management plays a larger role in the decision-making process as well. You may have experienced cost overruns, or failed projects, and project management has been enlisted to prevent things from going off the rails. Now they are responsible for successful project implementations. Time, cost, and scope management is part of how a value solution is defined and critiqued.

When the salesperson is aware of and understands project management's objectives, the two parties can work in a collaborative manner. Together, they can ensure everyone has a full understanding of what implementation will look like. Sales and project management actually share the same intentions. It behooves sales to help project managers to build strong business case with hard evidence and test assumptions. These two critically important elements are vital in qualifying the sales opportunity and ensuring the product is the right fit for the company. Teaming up to identify the correct information helps all parties involved.

WORKING IN TEAMS

Working with all of the stakeholders around the table increases the selling effort significantly. Most salespeople are not prepared to take this on because of the work involved, and sometimes there is pushback from the client. However, if they don't work with everyone at the table, the risk of losing the deal increases.

Be sure the solution you present meets the requirements of everyone involved. Show that you have considered what matters to them, that you understand their concerns, and more importantly, that you have properly qualified the opportunity. It's incumbent on the salesperson to make sure they are using the resources within the organization to ensure alignment across channels.

Within a team, there are always competing agendas. Everyone has different requirements and measurements, and the salesperson needs to be well aware of all of them. There may be a separate procurement process, as previously discussed, that will overlay all the stakeholders to ensure that a final decision of the stakeholders meets the policies of the organization. In the previous example, the IT manager is the person the salesperson will likely be working with, regardless of whether that person has the authority to make purchasing decisions.

There are circumstances where the salesperson does not have access to all the people who should be at the table. Getting to them can be a difficult and touchy process. You want to tread lightly so people are not insulted, or feel undermined. Most people make the mistake of trying to bypass the IT manager. They say things like, "I appreciate your time very much. Can you please introduce me to your boss or whoever the person is who has the final say?" Of course, that is going to do nothing except offend the IT manager and cause him to throw up defensive walls.

Instead of taking the "Who's the decision maker?" approach, simply open up the conversation with the IT manager to learn more about who is going to be involved. It's perfectly acceptable to start with a string of information-seeking questions, such as: "How have you handled similar projects in the past? For a project of this size, we can initially run a small trial." That suggestion usually leads to the discovery of important information.

The client might respond by saying, "If it goes over X size, we have a procurement and a project management team that needs to be involved." At that point, the salesperson can explore the size and structure of those additional teams. When you describe the *how*, the *who* is often revealed. For example, "John Smith is the head of procurement, and his team is made up of Joe, James, and Jimmy."

Likewise, if a project team is formed to implement a new system, talk to the manager about who is on the team and what their roles are. In this situation, I'll often say something along the lines of, "I have seen the project undertaken this way, which is in alignment with what I understand you would like to do. Does this idea fit with what you were thinking, and is that how you would tackle it?" Positioning it in that way prompts a conversation.

The manager might respond, "Yes, for the most part, that's how we do it, but Jimmy comes in at the end for quality control." Regardless, having the conversation helps you to identify roles and individuals.

Whenever the topic of process comes up, the people who will be involved naturally come up in the discussion. It's even possible to build awareness to the degree that you understand what is going on around the decision process and who the influencers are.

I always try to build that understanding out even further by looking for trigger dates. Start with the end in mind and work backward. "If we are going to have the system up and running by X date, what decisions need to be made, by whom, and by when? What processes need to occur for us to meet our shared launch goal date?" That gives you a clear timeline, in addition to a full list of who all the key players are.

Once you've run through a detailed conversation with the IT manager and have a complete picture, then you can ask for an introduction to the rest of the team. It's less off-putting than it would have been if you asked straight out of the gate. Now, you're engaged in their process and you want to do everything you can to facilitate it.

The manager might be protective of his team's time and give you a little bit of pushback. He might say, "They're busy. This is my job, and I can relay whatever questions you have to the rest of the team. I will get all the answers for you." It's all about how you treat the project manager and the respect you show him for his role.

I tackle pushback a few different ways. One of them is to say, "Because the rest of the team is involved in this process and they all have different roles, wouldn't it make sense to know up front what success looks like to them? It might vary slightly from your perspective as the IT manager, and we want this to be a winning solution for everyone. I would love to be able to answer their questions and explore how everyone can get the most out of this process."

Very rarely is this a straightforward discussion, because there are so many moving parts going on behind the scenes. There's never a clearly defined "way in" to meet all the stakeholders. Good, solid reasoning is a great place to start, though. Even if you can't get a face-to-face meeting, fifteen minutes on the phone could be enough to get a real sense of what matters to them.

SAMUEL SAYS: BE CLEAR ON WHO IS AT THE TABLE AND WHY.

As we're building the business case, there may well be some intangible soft evidence that can be built into hard evidence. Sometimes, we need to put numbers to those intangibles to make them more real. For example, they might fall just outside of the IT manager's realm, and therefore, they are not a high priority for him. Or they may lie in someone else's domain, and the IT manager is not even aware of them.

If you can present the numbers in a way that helps the IT manager build a business case, then you are one step closer to getting your sale through. The decision makers care about hard evidence, so keep those elements as your main focus.

BEST IN SHOW: WHO'S AT THE TABLE?

1. How is your client going to make a decision?

2. What is the client's process and timeline?

3. What is the expected completion dates and why?

4. Who is involved in the decision making?

   🏆 What are the individual roles?

5. What are the decision criteria?

6. How do the criteria differ for each stakeholder?

7. Identify the *who* and discuss the how.

CHAPTER 5

ROAM IN PACKS

There was always a pack of dogs running about on the vineyard. Sam was the newest member of a well-established crew who wandered over to check in, laze about in the sun, and sniff around. His status as an outsider was understood. There was a clear leader who always started a kangaroo or rabbit chase through the vineyards. There was one dog that opted out of the activities, especially if it was a hot day. He preferred to lie in the shade of a tree.

Each dog understood his or her role and job within the pack and, for the most part, got along harmoniously. Their little community worked because each dog did his or her part to contribute. Dogs, like people, are social animals, and they function well in an environment of cooperation where everyone understands what his or her contribution is. The strength of the unit comes from working together and meeting each other's expectations.

In the same vein, it's important to recognize your pack in a sales environment. There are two key elements to the pack mentality in sales: your allied partners and your clients. Both groups have different behavior dynamics and a separate breakdown of responsibilities.

ALLIED PARTNERS

When clients go through the buying process, they often consider multiple products or services. It's highly unusual for a big purchase to occur in isolation. For example, if someone is planning to put in a pool, that person would also need landscaping, fencing, and chemical and cleaning services. The pool involves far more than simply digging a hole in the ground.

The same scenario is true in the case of a large IT sale. For example, a software installation is likely to have a significant impact on the organization. Changes that affect people or processes require some advance groundwork as well as post-implementation follow-up. Perhaps change management services or hardware upgrades are necessary to accommodate the purchase.

Over time, you will find that you run into the same group of people who are at the job site facilitating the other arms of the transaction. Eventually, alliances are formed because you're all working toward a common end result, even though everyone is involved in the sale at different stages. In this type of situation, the leader of the pack is often the person the client started the conversation with. In the case of the pool example, it would be the installer and the allied services and all the other elements necessary to complete the project.

There's great value in establishing relationships with the people in your allied services pack. Sales and marketing efforts are more effective if you are working together. Often, the client will ask the pack leader for recommendations regarding the additional necessary services. It's helpful for the client if you have a list of people you've already worked with and trust to get the job done. Plus, it simplifies the experience for the client and can shorten the sales cycle.

When a team of allied service people are working together, they tend to share leads, opportunities, and information with each other. I was working on a software sale one time and ran into the guy who was handling the hardware piece. He pulled me aside to let me know there might be a delay due to a budgeting error on the client's end. The information allowed me to reevaluate the opportunity and respond accordingly. It saved a huge amount of time on my part. I was able to reprioritize what I spent my time on and update my sales forecast. His insight was valuable and helped boost my credibility within the organization. It helped to show that I care about accurate forecasting as much as I care about making a sale.

If your internal team is working in sync, the marketing team will qualify the lead and identify what prerequisites are necessary for a sale to go through. If there are a number of prepurchase steps or considerations, marketing usually outlines what those steps are and what products are needed.

For example, if you're in the business of selling backyard pools, the marketing team should inform the client about the required approval process and the ongoing maintenance costs. Otherwise, sales risks losing what they think are good opportunities because the client is underprepared. You don't want the client to abandon the idea of putting in a pool because he or she cannot meet the permit requirements or isn't prepared to meet the costs of ongoing maintenance. Marketing educates the client about costs and procedures before sales steps in. The clients must be ready and prepared to proceed.

Some organizations spend a lot of time developing allied sales channels, or packs, to make the sale as smooth as possible for the client. For example, in the previous case, the pool sales company might refer the client to other companies that can assist with the permit process or that supply the maintenance services.

The end goal is to help the client realize the total benefit of the solution being offered. Often this requires an educational component. Marketing will help to ensure that the client understands the process he or she needs to go through to solve the problem, as well who the necessary pack members should be.

From a sales perspective, allied relationships are crucial to ensuring a comprehensive flow of trade-specific information. It's worth getting involved in a few industry associations. They are a great source of market intelligence, new pack offerings, trends, issues, and insights. As marketing budgets have shifted online, industry organizations have suffered slightly, but they are still a powerful way to get a read on the market within the context of your specific field.

Don't overlook the value of the relationships you can build just by getting to know other people who share your challenges. Over a casual cup of coffee or a drink after work, coming together socially with the pack is a great way to share leads and other project-specific details. Perhaps someone has uncovered a useful piece of information that isn't necessarily important for their contribution but will have an impact on someone else's. Or perhaps one of your pack members has worked with the client previously and has some valuable acumen around specific constraints within the organization.

If the client trends are moving in a certain direction, it's worthwhile for the pack to meet and discuss. It's possible that three or four different pack members may have noticed certain behaviors or signals that caused them pause. When you're in a group setting, you can get your heads together and compare notes to reveal larger issues or roadblocks. Something that might take a salesperson six months to uncover can be revealed in a single afternoon. The shared information allows you to take actions you may not have even known to take.

For example, I was working with a number of data-center operators in Australia. The main thing this group of people talked about was cloud-based client solutions. Three years ago, the conversation was about leasing computer storage. In a relatively short period of time, the client requirement changed entirely.

If I had not been part of the conversation, my interactions with the clients would have been on outdated services. Because of the shared pack knowledge, we were able to adjust our marketing messaging accordingly. The sales-people were retained and updated on where the market was going, and they were able to offer relevant solutions to the clients' needs.

Relationships with allied partners can be cultivated in any number of ways. Typically, you'll meet your fellow pack members at the job site, the way Sam met his group at the vineyard. When you work on a project with someone more than once, the bond of a shared experience is formed. Take advantage of the fact that you've met other people on the same client premises, and actively seek out those who are involved in offering the same type of solutions.

Perhaps marketing has already identified who the best partners for the project might be and has tasked you, the salesperson, with initiating a relationship with them. In that case, a natural lead-in is to say, "Hey, Joe. We're trying to solve X problem for ABC Corp. If we have a relationship with your company, we can work together and share the business. It's a win-win. How can we collectively deliver a better experience for the client?" Most people are open to exploring ways to be more efficient through joint sales and marketing efforts.

CONTENT MARKETING 2.0

Consumers have gathered an awareness of the purpose of content marketing and have become more skeptical of it. They've started to view it as advertising and lead generation disguised as education with vendor bias. Content marketing is naturally biased. It often comes with a request for contact information, which in turn generates automated marketing e-mails that appear to be personalized.

It's only a matter of time before content marketing goes the same way as direct mail. Direct mail used to capture people's attention because the envelope was personalized. It didn't take long before people started to recognize it as junk mail or unsolicited advertising.

Specifically, I've noticed the drop-off in lead-nurturing efforts from HubSpot in the last few years. Initially, a downloaded white paper or e-book was followed up with personalized e-mails that addressed specific interests. HubSpot enjoyed such a favorable response that people took the time to acknowledge the automated e-mail as if it really were personalized. It seemed as if the senior consultant truly had taken the time to offer further information without an expectation of anything in return.

Unfortunately, this process of lead generating became an industry standard, and since then, the response rate has dropped significantly. People are no longer pleasantly surprised by the follow-up. Now they are skeptical and dismissive.

Today's best leads come from community and referrals, and the trend will only increase in years to come. Therefore, now is the time to actively nurture your own community. The old-school forums are still active, but Facebook has certainly taken a large part of the pie (or discussion). That's where people are learning about new products and services. Finding discussion groups is relatively easy, and there is no shortage of helpful videos and feedback.

THE CLIENT PACK

Just like allied team members, clients also have a tendency to travel in packs. It's important to understand and recognize the dynamics that surround client groups and how they interact so that you can most effectively approach them, both individually and collectively.

Today, it's easier than ever to track client behavior through Facebook, websites, and other online channels. When clients are thinking about making a purchase, they will usually consult one of the various online channels for feedback, information, or direction.

Marketing plays a key role in understanding client packs just as much as they do in identifying allied partner packs. Many organizations have engaged brand ambassadors to promote and advocate for the product or service. It's marketing's responsibility to be aware of who those influencers are within the client packs.

I wish social media was around when I was working at the family-owned and -operated vineyards. The owners worked like dogs. They slogged it out because of their passion for viticulture, winemaking, and the lifestyle of it all. They made a living and got by, but the old joke was: How do you make a small fortune from the wine industry? Start with a large fortune!

The problem was that the larger wine producers killed them. They had more resources and scalability, and their size allowed them to buy the resources cheaper. The small guys competed for ad space in the same magazines, but didn't get the same type of discounts. They paid for accounting and legal services, but without corporate incentives. They paid just as much as the larger producers, although it came out to be a much larger percentage of their sales that went to those expenses.

Selling the wine was challenging too. The small vineyards got locked out of the major supermarkets by the multinationals. If they sold through the cellar door, they had to be located on the main tourist routes. Often this meant being in close proximity to the major producers, which meant the land was more expensive. Eventually, most of the family operations sold out to the multinational winemakers because they simply couldn't compete.

Today, the landscape has changed dramatically. Small-vineyard family producers can find a community that appreciates their offering, and they can buy the resources they need from small-scale suppliers. Their customer base could be anywhere in the world. Often, their customers do the advertising for them online. The community is king these days, not the almighty advertising dollar.

THE "PREMIUM" CRAFT BEER MARKET

A similar phenomenon has played out in the craft beer market in the United States. In March 2016, *Fortune* reported that the craft beer market had grown 13 percent in the previous year. It was the eighth year of double-digit growth in the craft beer market, yet the overall beer market shrank marginally.

Some marketers attribute the growth to the fact that beer drinkers are willing to pay more for premium brands. That may be partially true; however, craft beers are not often associated with a "premium" classification. BMW, Louis Vuitton, and Moet Chandon are brands associated with *premium* in most people's minds. They are expensive, global, well known, and highly regarded. Many of them have a heritage that dates back a century or more, and they each have enjoyed brand dominance for decades.

So how does a brand-new, expensive, small-volume, single-location craft brewer earn the same "premium" classification as some of the world's best-known brands? *Premium* means more than just being a little bit more expensive than the market average. Community and connectivity bring new value to the retail equation.

The real reason the craft beer market is enjoying double-digit growth year over year is because of the community that has ridden up to support it. Yes, craft beer is more expensive than domestic mass-produced beer, but the craft beer consumers appreciate its value and taste and are willing to pay "premium" prices for it. Like any product or service, many of the craft beers on the market have earned their value standing. When customers get on board with a product's value, they are willing to pay for it.

The market must see the value in the product. The product, service, or beer must earn its value, and when that happens, customers are willing to pay a higher price. In the case of craft beers, the value may be in the fact that the beer is produced locally, employs local staff, and uses local ingredients. The value goes beyond simply being a refreshing-tasting beer. The value is the economic contribution the beer has for the local town and the people who live there.

Outside of the local value, people in a wider community might find their wants fulfilled by a product or service that satisfies other, intangible desires that product or service represents. Today, building and nurturing a community can be done far more cost-effectively than in years past, and in a manner that allows scalability in line with the business's resources.

The big players no longer necessarily have market dominance. Small companies are transparent, and consumers enjoy much greater visibility into the inner workings of their favorite brands and companies. People within a community can look for a unique set of features and share and compare in ways they couldn't before.

It's no longer necessary to occupy prime real estate along the main road for your business to have visibility. Online visibility to the desired target community is more than sufficient. It's also no longer necessary to have huge marketing and advertising budgets. Marketing can be done in a small and cost-efficient manner through Google and Facebook. Today's small-business owners are looking at a few dollars a day versus hundreds of thousands of dollars a year in promotion. Plus, because of various analytics tools, they know exactly what their return on investment is. They can experiment with different marketing messages every day instead of committing to three fixed messages over a long period of time and praying one of them resonates with the customers.

If you hear grumblings in the market about a shift to "premium" products, just take a closer look at what is really going on. Is it truly a shift to premium, or is it a shift in what value represents?

SAMUEL SAYS: COMMUNITY MARKETING IS MORE POWERFUL THAN CONTENT MARKETING.

Social listening is key to organizing, influencing, and facilitating client packs. Research and development ideas tend to result from paying attention to online client conversations, and they give the marketing department an opportunity to engage with the issues that clients are talking about. If there are complaints or comments that warrant interaction, the company can step in and take action and demonstrate that they are listening, aware, and care about problems.

There are several examples of client complaints on Twitter. For example, McDonald's uses Twitter to monitor client feedback and address complaints (@reachout_mcd). They use this handle to listen to, respond to, and engage with customers. Separating the complaints from the corporate page (@mcdonalds) was a smart strategy. If one comment grows into six, the issue escalates from an isolated incident to a threat to the entire brand. Social listening allows the company to get control of a situation before it gets out of control. Twitter, especially, has a tendency to unleash a pack-like mentality, but it also allows companies to get ahead of the issue.

Even if there isn't an immediate problem, social listening can help to identify areas that need improvement. It also allows the company to get a competitive advantage by conducting free market research. In the old days, companies organized focus groups and had their clients fill out surveys to get feedback. The research element was often contrived and didn't always yield completely honest responses.

A famous example of bad client intelligence happened about thirty years ago with Coca-Cola. They wanted to roll out a new recipe for the classic drink and modernize the taste of it. The market research indicated that consumers would love the new flavor, but when New Coke was rolled out in 1985, it was a complete disaster. The clients revolted because they didn't want a new flavor; they wanted the taste of traditional Coke Classic, which the company was forced to restore. It was a costly error and one that likely would not have happened in today's era of social listening.

When a company is involved with its client pack online, they are in a position to ask questions and receive feedback. The best part is that this opportunity is free and immediate. The previous methods of market research involved a huge investment of time, energy, and dollars as well as a long lag time. Also, when research occurs online, the clients are one step removed from the process. They're far more likely to share their honest feelings behind the screen than they are in a face-to-face situation. It is much easier to identify trends and test ideas instantly when you understand where your client pack is and what they are communicating to each other.

BEST IN SHOW: GROWING YOUR REACH

1. Network with professionals in related fields.

- 🏆 Who is in your pack?

- 🏆 Which industries are allied with yours?

- 🏆 What organizations should you be a member of to gain better insight into your clients?

- 🏆 Who do your clients engage with before, during, and after they interact with you?

2. Identify your client packs.

- 🏆 Where are your client packs, and what are they saying?

- 🏆 Where do they go to find and share information?

- 🏆 Who are the influencers?

- 🏆 What are their common issues or pain points?

- 🏆 Do your clients belong to any clubs or associations?

CHAPTER 6

WORK LIKE A DOG

Sam and I used to get up at the crack of dawn on the weekends and head over to the vineyard. Over time, he came to know the routine of the place. He could tell by the items that I gathered in the morning what the day had in store and what kind of fun lay ahead. He knew where we were going and what we would be doing based on specific triggers, such as the machinery we fired up or grapes being tossed in the crusher. Sam was always ready to go and excited to tackle whatever the day had in store.

His enthusiasm was infectious and motivated the entire team. It's hard to be grumpy when there's a four-legged fur ball bouncing around with excitement, even if you haven't had your coffee yet. My boss told me that things always got done faster when Sam was around. He lifted everyone's spirits in the morning and helped us all get out of our own way. From just a few telling movements, Sam was off and raring for a great day. He thrived on routine and activity; in fact, he sought it out.

The work for the day was dictated by the season and the weather. It also depended on what stage of the winemaking process we were in. There were plenty of side jobs that needed to be done, but the central focus was on producing the wine and getting it bottled, packaged, and ready for sale. The tasks became habit, and Sam had a good sense of those habits, routines, and seasons at the vineyards.

PLAN TO SUCCEED

Disciplined planning and executing is key to success in sales, just as the routine of the vineyard drove efficiency. Visualizing what lies ahead in the day has a big impact on productivity because willpower alone is not enough. There are many elements to the day in sales that can easily feel like a grind: responding to inquiries, calling people to follow up, and introducing yourself to potential new clients. Many people tend to avoid the activities they don't like, and then things quickly pile up.

Salespeople often fall into the trap of mistaking urgency for importance. Someone else's pressing matter is not necessarily your pressing matter. Being able to make the distinction and draw a line in the sand is critical for staying in control of your own workflow. The things on your list should always be your own priorities, not someone else's. This is why taking the time to plan and prepare is so helpful. When you know what to focus on, things will happen in the right order. You are less likely to get derailed.

Your own results are what count. If someone sends you an e-mail marked "urgent," you need to be able to assess the validity of the claim and determine where the issue falls in your own priorities. How will the contents of the e-mail impact what you are trying to achieve that day? Don't confuse activity with the desired outcome.

PUT YOURSELF IN CONTROL

Planning the week in advance is a critical step to successfully completely everything that needs to get done. Salespeople have a tendency to develop the unhealthy habit of being reactive as opposed to proactive. It's very easy to allow extenuating circumstances to dictate how your day will play out. Don't fall into the common trap of chasing your tail by answering every incoming phone call or e-mail if there are other things you need to do to promote your own agenda. Phone calls and e-mails can be distracting or demotivating to the point of inaction.

Instead, assign certain times of the day to do the tasks you typically put aside, and create a routine. Eventually, completing those tasks becomes a reflex instead of a chore. Slowly over time, they will require less energy to complete. You may even find yourself approaching them with enthusiasm.

The most effective way to become the master of your own productivity is by gaining control over your calendar and your to-do list. Visualize how you want your day and week to unfold. You are far more likely to approach the activities that lie ahead with enthusiasm, as Sam did, when you know what lies ahead. You have the power to choose between the grind and the thrill of the chase. Which road is going to have the most positive outcome for you?

SAMUEL SAYS: PLANNING AND DISCIPLINE ARE KEY TO SALES SUCCESS.

Find a system that works for you. Early in my sales career, I decided to use a CRM (customer relationship management) system for my sales efforts. It helped to keep me on top of what I had to do and where deals and conversations were in the process. With little effort at all on my part, CRM also helped me to create a sales pipeline and focus my day-to-day activities.

Many salespeople resist CRM because it's often introduced as a management tool, instead of a sales tool. It can seem like an inconvenience when presented incorrectly. The real value of CRM is when it is used collaboratively among sales, marketing, and customer service to capture customer information. It saves the clients from having to explain their story every time they speak to someone new at the company. Plus, it makes them feel valued and understood.

CRM allows an organization to capture the complete life cycle of the client. It tracks every engagement and response; triggers follow-ups, phone calls, and e-mails; and keeps all the information organized. You don't have to stay on top of all the details and think about what you need to do next if you use a reliable CRM system. It is an invaluable tool to manage your pipeline and productivity so you can have more constructive conversations and save time.

I spend the last few minutes of each workday preparing for the next. I'll sit down and make a list of who I need to call, who is waiting for a response for me, and what specific tasks need to be completed. Then, I'll look at my calendar and schedule the time I need to accomplish those tasks. This exercise gives me far more control over how I spend my time. Plus, when I get to my desk the next day, I can immediately start in on the day's activities. I'm clear on the desired outcome for the day, and I am driving my own agenda. Because I feel as if I'm in control (and I am), I have a far more positive perspective on the day and, as a result, am more productive.

Please note that I am not suggesting you get into the habit of creating outrageously long to-do lists. This is a common problem and one that can actually unhinge the best of intentions. A mile-long to-do list has been proven to make people less constructive with their time. Plus, if you're using CRM, you won't need to worry about a to-do list!

When you define the outcomes you'd like to achieve for the day or the week, you'll find that there are considerably less desired results than there are tasks. Focus on the big picture, in which there are only three or four major things to accomplish, instead of every single phone call and e-mail that needs attention. This process is called "chunking," and it involves creating blocks of activity.

For example, you may need to do the following:

1. Create a tender.
2. Follow up on leads.
3. Talk to marketing about support measures.

You have three clear chunks of things you are trying to achieve, and you are clear on what they are. The objective is to avoid being overwhelmed by looking at your day or week in small, manageable, bite-size pieces. When you're focused on outcomes, your to-do list naturally writes itself.

Assessing risk and close dates leads to further clarity. For example, if there is a tender report due, the assignment comes with a clear and fixed deadline. Most organizations don't cut too much slack around it; therefore, the deadline tells you it is an important action. There's a high risk around not completing it, because other important steps will be ignored, such as the creation of the bid. Naturally, the tender report needs to be at the top of the priority list. Oftentimes, deadlines help to identify the items you should focus on.

What can you do today to move a deal forward? Putting your attention toward solving a client objection is generally a more effective use of time than e-mailing the latest company brochure. Be mindful of your actions, and think about how they will lead you closer to the desired outcome. When your focus is on moving deals forward, your actions have greater value.

Given the volume of distractions in today's world, follow-up is a vitally important action on a salesperson's agenda. Statistics show that it takes at least six attempts at contact before a client engages with a salesperson. Awareness around typical client behavior makes follow-up less arduous. If you're feeling ignored, recognize that there is a process unfolding within the client's subconscious. They are likely trying to get clarity on the issue before they responding to your follow-ups. Keep at it, and don't get discouraged.

Many salespeople give up way too easily when they don't get a prompt response. There is a fine line between being perceived as an annoyance and being perceived as helpful. Be sure that all of your communication with the client delivers some sort of value to them.

Ideally, by the time you have a lead, it's been prequalified by marketing. There should be some context for reaching out to the person. You should have, at the very least, a vague idea about what the client's issues are and what he or she is looking for to solve the problem. Background knowledge helps to set the stage for your follow-up, to the degree that you are confident enough to reach out and say, "Hi, Joe. I understand you are having an issue with X. Given the work we have done in the past for XYZ Corp, we have great insight into this area. I am happy to share what we've learned with you. Give me a call back to discuss."

Alternatively, the marketing team may have produced a document that outlines the client's considerations. Each step of the client interaction needs to be thought through carefully. It is more effective to reach out and say, "We took the liberty of outlining some of the risks we've seen other clients experience and thought this report would be helpful to you."

There will always be an initial education component to the interaction, so continued communication with marketing is necessary. They can help to produce informational pieces, brochures, videos, and Web content that will add value for the client. Plus, marketing can gauge the level of interest based on open rates, click-throughs, and other critical online data.

LEAD AND LAG MEASURES

A key task of the sales management team is to drive predictable sales results. Yet, most sales organizations are looking at the wrong business metrics to be able to influence and predict the results. Unfortunately, most reporting systems are built to meet the requirements of the accounting and financial team, not the sales team. Sales management needs to develop their own set of metrics, which are very different than what is readily available from within the organization.

Sales management tends to focus on results after the fact: sales revenue, gross profit margin, or stock turns. These are all historical measurements indicating past performance. Management can't do anything about the result or affect the outcome. When the results don't hit the target, then management goes about the task of guessing how to improve the key measures for the next period. What exactly needs to be changed or what action or inaction that led to the performance is unclear.

Most business reporting systems are designed to capture these historical metrics, which are called lag measures. They are generally simple to record, monitor, and report.

Lead measures, on the other hand, are the actions or actives that influence the lag measure. For example, if a key lag measure for a business was the sales revenue for the month, the lead measures the influence of the lag measure, such as the number of sales leads, sales calls, customer appointments, or quotes provided to customers. These are all lead measures that influence or make the lag measure, sales revenue, predictable.

To capture and monitor lead measures tends to require more work and analysis than lag measures, and as a result, a lot of organizations simply do not do it. Yet, if management wants a predictable outcome or to influence the results, they need to identify lead measures and monitor the results.

Thankfully, as CRM systems have become more commonplace, it has become less challenging to capture lead measures. Management needs to develop the discipline to work on the leading indicators of success. Most organizations have an understanding of their success ratio, such as the number of quotes issued and sales calls made. These are simple sales metrics that build the opportunity pipeline. For example, a company might win 30 percent of the projects it bids on. If the company wants to win $100,000 worth of business, it needs to bid on $333,000 worth of work. Should the sales numbers fall short, the company can look at both the success rate and the value of the business bid to address the sales shortfall for the next period.

A further example of the application of lead and lag measures is the desire to lose weight. The lag measure—standing on the scale—is easy to measure. Standing on the scale to see how much you weigh is not terribly taxing. Losing weight is another matter altogether. The number on the scale isn't necessarily going to help you to lose the weight, but focusing on the right exercise and diet is the specific action necessary to achieve the goal. Sales works the same way.

If management wants more predictable outcomes, they need to focus on the actions that drive the results. If the lead measures are not monitored, it's impossible to understand what areas need improvement. Establishing the lead measures for your business is necessary to move deals forward, which dictates how you spend your time, which in turn gives you more control over your day.

Unfortunately for productivity, most organizations still focus on cold hard dollars. Everyone on the sales team has a number they need to achieve, but what it takes to get to that number is often glossed over, and it certainly isn't monitored. Get real about the data. Measure it, and put as much focus on lead measures as you do lag measures. Again, enlist the help of marketing because they have the tools to capture the statistics necessary.

DISCIPLINE YOUR PACK

Just as you would train a dog, you also need to train those around you to be efficient through structure and good habits. When others around you know why they're doing something, they'll start participating with you and also build good habits.

Remember Sam's enthusiasm at the beginning of each workday at the vineyard? That's how you want your teammates and coworkers to behave as well. For example, I used to sit down on a regular basis with the marketing and client service teams. Every Friday afternoon, I pulled key numbers and metrics for them, and we discussed where specific deals were in the sales process. We reviewed the status of each deal, and we filled each other in on what was happening, where the roadblocks were, and what particular issues the client might be facing.

This weekly meeting became a routine, and we all looked forward to it. It was a chance to catch up, regroup, and strategize. A few things happened as a result. The in-house client service pack started to prepare for the meeting. Even if they simply made mental notes during conversations that took place during the week, they knew what type of information I was going to ask for and the types of interactions that were of interest.

The meetings progressed to the point where I no longer asked questions; the pack just automatically knew what I'd want to know. In short order, Suzy from client service would stand up and say, "Steve, here are six things that are going on with XYZ Corp. What are your thoughts?"

Then, in no time at all, instead of me telling them what to say back to the client, Suzy from client service became conditioned to already know what I would say. She was empowered enough by the structure of the routine to get back to the client *before* the meeting and move the sales process one step closer to completion.

I followed the same procedure with the marketing team. We established a time and a day for a weekly update meeting. I set the agenda, and the marketing team grew to know what my expectations were. They knew exactly what type of information was important, and they anticipated the delivery of that information by being prepared. They didn't report to me, and I had no direct control over them; they simply recognized the value in what I wanted to know. Once they understood that I was working with them toward a common organizational objective, they got on board with enthusiasm.

Just as client service had, marketing also began to prepare the content for the weekly meetings over the course of the week. They started to pay closer attention to the number of leads, where the leads came from, and what programs were effective. If the date wasn't in line with my expectations, they took corrective measures and adjusted their processes to have a better outcome.

You don't have to be a sales manager to have influence. If the people you work with understand what is important to you, habits begin to form around how they approach tasks and activities. It doesn't take long either. When people know that you intend to meet weekly to discuss a fixed agenda, the behaviors that support that agenda follow suit. People naturally get on board to assist you in your process, and conversations that cover pertinent issues ensue.

THE CLIENT PACK NEEDS TRAINING TOO

We've all had meetings canceled or postponed at the last minute. It helps if the reason for the meeting is made clear in advance. Knowing what the discussion points are helps to prevent cancellations, but sometimes customers can be tricky to pin down. They hardly ever answer the phone or respond to e-mails when *we want* something. Therefore, calls and e-mails need to be *about them*. They need to understand from the outset that the salesperson is simply responding to what they have shown an interest in by way of marketing efforts. In the past, salespeople always acknowledged and thanked customers for their effort and time. Once a meeting time had been set up, people tended to keep it.

I grew up before mobile phones. As a young teenager, if I wanted to meet up with my friends, we had to set a time and place in advance. Under the clock at the railway station was a popular spot. We planned to meet days in advance, and we stuck to those plans religiously. We were on time because there was really no other option. There was no way to send a message if someone was running late. If someone was late, we just waited and waited for them to show up; everyone understood the need to get there on time.

Later on in life, I took that mentality into the workplace. I set up meetings with clients in small country towns in advance of traveling there. If I had met the customer before and said I would be in town, I always got the meeting. The customer understood the effort I was making and knew I wouldn't be making the trip without a good reason, such as my having something new to show them. Even in the city, my customers usually kept their meetings with me. If someone needed to cancel, they did so several days in advance.

Now, given our instant-gratification lifestyle and instant communication, people seem to cancel with increased frequency and closer to the scheduled time slot. Many people are more than happy to cancel at the last minute or not show up at all. If something else comes up, they don't usually say, "Sorry, I have a previous engagement that I scheduled weeks ago." Instead, they make a game-time decision about which meeting is more important, which only emphasizes the fact that customers must be very clear on what you want to meet with them about and why. They must understand what they can expect to get out of the meeting and what you expect from them as well. Setting expectations *in advance* is critical.

HOW TO OPEN CONVERSATIONS, MEETINGS, AND PRESENTATIONS

Although not every meeting or conversation requires an advance agenda, the purpose of the interaction needs to be clear on both sides. The customer needs to understand that at the end of the meeting, you want and expect a decision. Meetings are much easier to get if the customer is clear on the purpose from the outset.

Start with the end in mind: What do you want the customer to say, do, or decide? Try opening the conversation with one of these examples:

- "I'd like to explore if our solution makes sense for your business and determine if we should meet another time to look at it in further detail." This scenario suggests a transition from an initial phone conversation to a face-to-face meeting.
- "At our last meeting, you raised a number of issues around the short-comings of our solution compared to our competitor. I'd like to address them one by one and get a better understanding of what you need to see or experience to put those concerns aside."
- "You mentioned last week that we need to finalize pricing. I'd like to walk through that with you in our meeting and see if we can come to an agreement on a price that will allow us to proceed with the project."

It helps to have a system of meeting confirmation, so the client understands and appreciates the value of your time. Like anything else, it just takes a little training and up-front expectation setting.

For example, I used to work for an IT company. New product rollouts occurred with some regularity, and I developed a system to gauge client interest by establishing a routine. Every quarter, I had a conversation with the clients and asked them what type of projects had (1) been guaranteed, (2) were slated for funding, and (3) would potentially get funding down the road.

I repeated this line of questioning every quarter for a year until it got to the point that the clients just told me what they had budgeted for the quarter. In very little time, the clients themselves were disciplined to the degree that they knew what I would ask and immediately provided me with the answers.

Not all meetings and conversations require an agenda, but the purpose needs to be clear to both sides. The customer needs to understand you want something at the end of the meeting—a decision. To help them with this understanding, make your expectations clear at the outset of the discussion. Start with the end in mind. For example: "I'd like to walk through the pricing structure today and see if we can come to an agreement that will allow us to proceed with the project."

Training the pack in sales and marketing is no different than the way Sam was trained at the vineyard. He was able to visualize what lay ahead and anticipate it with enthusiasm. By establishing a routine and setting expectations, in no time at all, the pack learns to predict what's coming and behaves accordingly.

Salespeople need to understand that habits endure when willpower runs out. Good organizational behaviors are the bedrock of sustainable success. If they are able to spend a few minutes at the end of each day to visualize what tomorrow will bring, they are one step closer to achieving the desired outcome. Prioritizing and chunking tasks is key. Set yourself up to win with effective planning.

BEST IN SHOW: MAKING YOUR TIME WORK FOR YOU

1. Take the time to chunk your to-do list.

🏆 Establish a daily wind-down habit of planning for tomorrow.

2. Follow up productively.

🏆 How do you add value to your follow-ups?

🏆 How can you best be of service to your clients?

🏆 Build valid reasons to follow up into your business based on the questions that are commonly generated at certain points of the sales process.

3. Get marketing to work for you.

🏆 Identify lead measures that contribute to your desired outcomes.

🏆 Can marketing assist with capturing the numbers around those measurements?

CHAPTER 7

STOP PLAYING FETCH

As a German shepherd/collie mix, Sam was a working dog. He was always active and constantly looking for something to do or chase. He viewed everyone who came to the cellar sales at the vineyard as a potential playmate. Weekends were the busiest times, and new people were always stopping by.

Whenever someone drove up, Sam grabbed his favorite, filthy tennis ball and dropped it at their feet the minute they stepped out of the car. Most people thought he was wonderful and clever when they first encountered him. They'd oblige him and give the ball a toss. The walk from the parking lot to the cellar sales was about one hundred meters, and Sam tried to get in as many throws as he could while the person made their way to the door.

Little did the unsuspecting visitor know, after the first throw, Sam would be at their side like glue until they could disappear safely into the cellar. The cuteness of this game wore off by the third or fourth throw as the ball collected dirt and slobber. Sam didn't notice or care that he was pestering the visitors. He was singularly focused on his objective. The only thing he cared about was the ball. The poor visitor would try to get a hold of the ball with two fingers or kick it away so not to have to touch the gross thing.

By Sunday, Sam's paws were often bleeding from playing this never-ending, one-sided game of fetch. He didn't care or notice, because all he wanted was someone to engage with him and play. Despite the obvious discomfort, he would chase the ball as long as someone was there to throw it for him. After a while, people didn't want to play anymore, and they could see the state of his paws. They hid the ball to avoid further injury, but Sam would get a stick or a rock, or anything that he could retrieve. Not only was he annoying, he was a sad sight.

CHASING THE BALL

The same scenario can unfold in a sales environment. The initial phone conversation or in-person meeting goes well. The lead is pleasant and seems interested in the product. The salesperson leaves the exchange feeling positive and thinking, "Well, that went well! I think there's a real opportunity here." But then the lead goes quiet. The salesperson can't understand how or why the person went from seeming interested to suddenly unavailable. Does this sound familiar?

Good salespeople understand the importance of follow-up. Presumably there are action items that need to be addressed on each side. The salesperson calls the lead, reminds him of the great conversation or meeting, and inquires about his readiness to move forward. Oftentimes, the lead responds by saying, "Oh, I haven't had a chance to read your material. Please get back to me in a few weeks." Or, "We're not ready to move ahead at this time, but why don't you try me next quarter." This response is what I refer to as "throwing the ball." The lead is indulging the salesperson, but doesn't have any real interest in playing the game. He is politely trying to make the salesperson go away, even if it's for just a few days or weeks.

Then, a few weeks later or the next quarter, the salesperson tries to approach the lead again. Many times the lead says, "Oh, thanks for calling. I haven't had the time to go through the information, but it occurs to me that I can't review it thoroughly without a costing proposal. Could you please draw one up for me to look at?" He's tossed the ball again.

The salesperson, naturally, thinks this is an excellent step in the right direction. They pour their time and energy into putting a proposal together and tell their sales manager that the deal is progressing very well. Then, weeks or months later, the salesperson catches the client on the phone. He still hasn't looked at the materials, but he thinks the proposal is too high. He asks the salesperson to put together some new numbers, and the whole cycle repeats itself. All of those extra requests from the client are just like the visitors at the vineyard. They keep throwing the ball and hoping eventually the salesperson will tire out and give up.

As salespeople, we don't want to be like Sam in a one-sided game of fetch, doing all the work, and bleeding from exertion. We need to be aware of the client's investment in the process. Having a million balls in the air doesn't mean deals are advancing. Don't keep chasing whatever the client throws your way and hope that it translates to a sale. You'll wind up licking your wounds with nothing to show for them.

There must be a meeting of the minds and a joint, vested interest for a deal to go through. You'll know a client is truly interested when he is willing to contribute time and resources to moving forward. If the client has put together a project team, properly evaluated the issues, or formed a business case, then he is serious. You are both heading in the same direction.

The salesperson needs to be able to tell the difference between genuine interest and playing the game. Pay attention to the red flags, and whatever you do, don't get into the bad habit of throwing the ball for yourself. I've seen this happen a few times, and it's a sad sight indeed.

You know you're in dangerous territory if you find yourself saying, "Would you like me to put together a proposal for you?" Or, "Can I develop a full-scale project plan for you?" You may think you are suggesting a logical next step, but if the client is not on the same page, you're only making extra work for yourself unnecessarily. You just made it easy for the client to delay even further. The client no longer has to worry about brushing you off politely, or responding to your phone calls, e-mails, or texts.

SAMUEL SAYS: THE CLIENT NEEDS TO BE INVESTED IN THE SALES PROCESS.

Take care to ask the correct questions when engaging with your clients. If a problem exists today, surely it has been around for a while, and it's your job to find out what the roadblocks are. For example, an enthusiastic IT manager may very badly want to purchase a new software tool. Find out if he has talked to anyone about this issue before. If so, who? Why didn't he move forward at the time? Were there budgetary constraints? Always ask, "Why now and why not before?"

The response may be something along the lines of, "Yes, I did raise this issue eighteen months ago. My operations director knocked it down because there were four other company priorities ahead of mine that needed to be addressed first." It's important to get a sense of how visible the issue has been within the company and for how long. Then ask, "So what's changed? How are things different today than they were eighteen months ago?" Make sure that you are speaking to the people who have the most invested in the outcome. It's important to understand that it is not one single person; there are going to be multiple stakeholders involved. This relates to identifying who the top dog is, which we discussed in chapter 4.

PUT THE BALL IN THEIR COURT

If you do find yourself in the position of chasing a deal in circles, try to determine the root cause of the holdup. Instead of ignoring the fact that you're getting the runaround, address it head-on. It's perfectly acceptable to say to the client, "Joe, I'm confused. Do I understand correctly that if XYZ problem is resolved, we can move forward? Do you see it the same way?"

For the benefit of both the salesperson and the client, the issues need to be placed squarely on the table. That way, they can be dealt with. These types of conversations can be intimidating, but they need to be had, and the client needs to provide you with the proper response. Ignoring the problem is only going to delay the inevitable, and it's just a matter of time before the deal dies on the vine.

There are often sales circumstances that require a long list of prerequisites in order for the deal to go through. I look for those things in the early stages of the conversation with the client so that I may speak to them intelligently. For example, consider the process of building a house. It's fun to talk to the contractor and the architect to design the house of your dreams. People get enthusiastic about planning where the rooms should go and picking out tile for the bathrooms. The permitting and permissions part of the process, on the other hand, can be less exciting.

In this building example, you cannot have the house unless you go through the unpleasant, costly, and time-consuming permitting process. Few people want to think about the logistics behind the dream house, but they're a reality. It's the contractor's responsibility to detail the entire scope of the project.

In some cases, it may be necessary to give the client homework, which puts the ball in his court if he wants to move forward. For example, IT integration typically involves some degree of interruption to the business. For the sale to be successful, the salesperson needs to acknowledge the interruption and what it means for the business. She also needs to have a clear plan for how the interruption will be dealt with. This is an opportunity to gauge how serious the client is about moving forward. The client will have to make a clear demonstration of their commitment.

The project may require additional resources or outside consulting. It's possible that the business needs to shut down for a few days. These things cost money. If the client is willing to absorb the cost for the prerequisite steps, manage the business interruption, and develop a plan, they have indicated their commitment to the project. If not, then simply say to the client, "You're not quite ready for implementation. Why don't we talk again once you've dealt with the required change process?" This makes it clear that the onus is on them and frees you up to move on to other things.

WHEN TO DISENGAGE

You need to be sensitive to how much time you are giving each client. Many salespeople get caught up in the chase with the false assumption that the sale is advancing. This leads to inflated forecasts and inaccurate reporting up the chain of command.

Ask yourself: Is the client as committed to the outcome as you are to the sale? If they truly believe in the value of the solution and the need to implement it in the near future, they will show their commitment by investing time or resources. If they don't contribute to the process, the project won't proceed. In which case, hand the issue back to the client and let them know what you need to see from their end.

Don't leave yourself vulnerable to reprimands from your sales manager. He or she might become irritated by how much time and extra resources you've devoted to a lead with nothing to show for it. Then you'll become frustrated, but worst of all, other opportunities have been neglected.

There's only so much time in the day, and the best use of your time is to focus on the clients who actually show a commitment. Plus, there are more effective ways of staying in touch with your clients than jumping through hoops. Make a note to follow up with them periodically and be clear about your process.

The last thing you want is to be viewed as an annoying salesperson. That's no way to build trust and confidence. In fact, relentless persistence undermines those critical relationship-building elements. If the client is not ready to move forward, position yourself as a trusted ally and a resource of information, instead of a pain in the neck. There are many ways to go about this, but the most effective way is to refer back to the education piece. Help the client to understand the process, as well as what needs to happen before and after implementation. Provide them with relevant information and case studies.

Continued education accomplishes several things at once. It keeps the lines of communication open. It helps the client make better-informed decisions and get clarity on the issues they may face. Best of all, you're establishing a rapport in an organic, genuine, and cost-effective manner. It demonstrates that you are the leader in this particular area and that you are the best choice to achieve the desired outcome.

BEST IN SHOW: KNOWING WHEN TO SAY WHEN

1. **The client needs to be fully invested in the process.**

   🏆 What specific investments do your clients need to enable the sale?

2. **Be aware of issues that may have come up for your client around the solution in the past.**

   🏆 What were the specific roadblocks, and have they been addressed internally?

   🏆 What has changed between then and now?

3. **Vague answers won't get the job done. Press for solid solutions, figures, timelines, and whatever else you need to move the sale forward.**

   🏆 What are the prerequisites the client needs to tackle before purchasing your solution?

   🏆 Have you addressed those prerequisites during your sales conversations?

CHAPTER 8

HOW MUCH IS THAT DOGGY IN THE WINDOW?

Little kids absolutely loved Sam. They all wanted to take him home with them. With a laugh, I'd tell the parents they too could have a mutt like Sam for just twenty dollars. That's how much he was advertised for in a small mention in the paper.

That number stuck in my friend's mind when he and his son were walking down the street one day and they passed a pet shop. The boy spotted a small, white fluffy dog in the window and begged his father to go inside the shop to find out more about it.

The father obliged, thinking this particular dog was not a bad pick. He was small, very cute, and didn't appear capable of doing too much damage to the house. In fact, he looked kind of like Sam might have as a puppy.

The first thing my friend asked the shopkeeper was how much the dog cost. The shopkeeper told him the dog was $800. They got into a conversation about the cost of the other dogs in the shop, and it turned out that all the other dogs were a fraction of the price. My friend said, "Hang on a second. How is it that the dog we're interested in is so much more than the other dogs that will surely grow to be three times the size?"

The shopkeeper explained that the dogs were priced by breed. My friend thought they should be priced by size because larger dogs cost more to care for; they eat more and take up more space. He felt a dog that would grow to be a fraction of the size should cost a fraction of the price. The debate went on for some time. The shopkeeper attempted to educate my friend about the fine qualities of the specific breed, and my friend maintained that the price should be based on size.

During the course of their circular argument, the shopkeeper failed to recognize that breeding didn't matter to my dad or his son. They had no understanding of or appreciation for pedigree, temperament, or breed-specific characteristics. They were just looking for a good family dog that would fit into their household—not a showpiece. My friend was so frustrated by the exchange that he left the shop, dragging his son along, who was having a fit because they were leaving without the dog.

On the whole, it was a very unpleasant experience for everyone. Had the shopkeeper stopped to consider why the pair walked into the shop to begin with, the story might have had a much happier ending. Instead, he was fixated on the value of that particular dog. If he had practiced active listening, he would have heard what was important to my friend: price, size, and adaptability into the home. He could have easily sold him another dog that fit those specific requirements.

HOW IS VALUE EARNED?

The value of a product or a service lies entirely in the eyes of the client. It's not the price tag or a margin placed on the cost of production; it's the significance of the solution to the client's problem or need.

Early in my career, one of my clients was a major Australian health insurance company. When the government mandated life insurance coverage, my client was faced with a flood of member paperwork to process within a fixed time frame. They were using an old mainframe system that they maintained internally, and it was about to fall apart. They asked if we could do the processing for them, even though the company I worked for offered data capture solutions, a completely different service. Nevertheless, I was enthusiastic and immediately agreed.

When I spoke to the home office about what I'd agreed to, they sat down to price out the cost of the job. It had an enormous price tag attached to it, and I was told, "There's no way the client will pay this amount." I prepared to go back and deliver the bad news. When I got there, the service manager started telling me about his internal constraints and how much it would cost them to do the processing themselves.

He quoted me a figure that was five times the amount we had priced the job to be! I walked into the meeting prepared to talk myself out of a sale when the client desperately needed our services. In fact, our price was a great ROI for them, and it was just the income boost we needed to open a Sydney office. It was a powerful lesson that the value of a product or service is in the eye of the beholder, not the salesperson. We cannot assume we know how badly a client needs what we're offering or how important the solution is to their functionality.

SAMUEL SAYS: THE SOLUTION HAS TO EARN ITS VALUE.

The features and benefits the client is looking for need to come from them, not the salesperson. By the time the price comes up, the salesperson should have already established a list of features the client is looking for and what issues need to be resolved or benefits delivered. He will have uncovered the impact the solution he is selling will have on the business and built the case. There's tangible, concrete evidence around what value is going to be delivered. From there, the salesperson is working with hard information, rather than assumptions.

PRICE OBJECTIONS: ARE THEY LOGIC- OR VALUE-BASED?

If pricing is an issue, it becomes imperative for the sales-person to circle back and redefine the value of the product or service to the client. Always, drill down into how the client derived the number in his or her head. It had to come from somewhere: peers online, other clients, or comparison-shopping. If your conversations with the client have been detailed and thorough, your price should be within a 10 percent margin of the figure they have in mind. Ideally, by following an in-depth sales process, you will avoid sticker shock altogether. The goal is to be on the same page from start to finish.

Get the price issue on the table early. Very often the client will ask about cost before the solution has been defined. If you're not on the same page, test the client's price range. It's perfectly acceptable to respond with something along the lines of, "Given what you want to achieve, our clients have spent between X and Y. Do you see yourself in that range?" If the answer is yes, great, you can move on. If not, start drilling into where their number came from.

It's not uncommon for the directive to come from the pro-curement department, who are trained to balk. Everyone in that section of the business has a reflex tendency to say, "You need to sharpen your pencil and come back with a better price." Some salespeople are so anxious to make

HOW MUCH IS THAT DOGGY IN THE WINDOW?

Customers see themselves spending between X and Y.

Do you see yourself in that range?

IF NOT, YOU FALL INTO TWO BOWLS

LOGIC ARGUMENT

"That's all we have left in the budget."

"That's what we allocated for it"

"That's my spending limit."

VALUE ARGUMENT

"It's not worth it."

"I can get it for less."

"You cannot deliver the promise."

"Competitor solution is better."

ASK THE CUSTOMER

"What should we do?"

(Hand the issue back to the customer.)

"What particular concern do you have?"

"Why do you feel that way?"

"What do you need to hear or see to change your viewpoint?"

the sale that they do actually come back with a significant discount, which is not advised. It shows desperation and devalues your own solution.

When discussing price, get specific about how much each part of the process costs and see if you can identify which areas are out of alignment with expectations. Get into a real discussion by saying, "We need to reevaluate the scope of the project. If we are going to be able to deliver what you are looking for at a lower price, we need to examine the various components and see what, if anything, can be pulled."

Going through the exercise of examining the cost of each part of the project oftentimes serves to highlight the value. If the client wants a discount, this conversation gives you the opportunity to discuss the importance of each part and how it contributes to their desired outcome.

If you're at this stage of the sales process, and the deal is in danger of falling through, there are a few key elements that need to be examined. It's possible you've completely missed a critical piece of information during the qualification step, in which case you need to revisit earlier conversations and get to the heart of the matter.

Establish what the client sees as constituting value, and work through their priorities. This can take some digging, especially if they've been tight-lipped about it up until now. Be patient and keep delving until you've identified the problem, as well as the anticipated benefit from the client's perspective. Nine times out of ten, when priorities are defined, the salesperson and the client can agree on value.

There is also the possibility that the client has seen something else on the market at a better price. There will always be cheaper options out there, and you need to be prepared for how to handle large price discrepancies. How is your solution superior to the competition? Are you looking at an "apples to apples" comparison? What are the core differences in your offerings, and how can you position your solution as the better choice?

A price objection tends to fall into one of two buckets: it's either a logic argument or a value argument. You need to be prepared to tackle both obstacles. If it's a logic argument, pass it back to the client to identify priorities. If it's about value, explore the reasons and address accordingly.

I was working on a software sale, and the process was unfolding nicely. We'd established early on that the client wanted to invest both time and resources into the project. We were within a suitable price range, the final project scope had been written and delivered, and we were all ready to go. Suddenly, the project stopped dead in its tracks. The client went dark on us and stopped taking our calls. A fabulous relationship turned cold overnight, and we couldn't figure out what the problem was.

Eventually, I was able to get the client on the phone. He informed me that he had a $20,000 price limit on pilot projects. We had come in at $25,000, so we knew we were on the high end. What we failed to understand was that $20,000 was the hard limit, and he couldn't go a penny over. Behind the scenes, he had been scrambling to come up with more money but was unable to do so. Instead of clearly communicating his limitations, he went silent. Once we understood the problem, we simply deferred a part of the solution that wasn't critical for impact and proceeded with the balance of the project.

The implementation was a success, and it actually led to a much larger sale down the road. Had we not been persistent about trying to understand why this project got derailed suddenly, we would have lost the whole deal. It would have been easy to blame it on the client and say he got cold feet. We all would have lost out if we'd chosen that path. The client would have missed out on a solution to their business issue, and we would have missed out on the initial and then the subsequent sale.

Oftentimes, logistical issues embarrass the people in procurement. They tend to clam up if there are limitations on their authority, even if there is a well-established relationship at stake. If a deal is in danger of being tabled at the eleventh hour, I always hunt around for the problem because there's often an easy fix.

You have to be sensitive to the type of company you're dealing with. For example, if it's a U.S.-based company, I'll say, "Listen, are you facing end-of-year budgetary constraints?" Australian companies are governed by a financial year that ends on June 30. Finance faces end-of-year in October. Whether the issue is financial or not, asking pointed questions helps to get to the root cause of the problem. You can't always trust the client to give you the straight story, but there is likely some sort of logical answer.

When the disparity is logic- or value-related, the important thing to remember is to keep the lines of communication as open as possible. When you know what the real problems are, you can usually find a solution.

BEST IN SHOW: UNDERSTANDING VALUE

1. The solution needs to earn its value.

🏆 What elements of your solution deliver value to the client?

🏆 Do you understand the client's priorities, and does the deal reflect them?

🏆 What benefits will the client receive, or what problems will be solved with your solution?

2. Conduct price discussions early in the sales cycle.

🏆 Have you tested the range?

🏆 Where does the client's number come from?

🏆 What does the range say about key issues, concerns, and solution priorities?

3. Know how to address price objections later in the sale cycle.

🏆 What issues is the price objection covering up?

🏆 Are the objections value- or logic-based?

CHAPTER 9

IN THE DOGHOUSE

At the vineyard and around our house, Sam understood there were certain areas he shouldn't be. The winemaker didn't want him in the winery for safety reasons; the housekeeper didn't want him in the house for cleanliness reasons; and the bookkeeper didn't want him underfoot in the office. He knew where he was permitted and what areas were off-limits. If he wandered into one of the areas he was not allowed, the result was predictable: he was sent to the doghouse until further notice. It didn't take Sam long to figure out that if he wanted to be a part of the action and roam with the pack, he needed to remember who objected to him being where and stay within his boundaries.

Sam played by the rules. He saw people go in and out of the off-limit areas and watched the activity from outside. He knew breaking the rules wasn't worth the risk of being sent to the doghouse and being excluded. He only made the same mistake once or twice before the predictability of the outcome was established in his mind.

THE FIVE OBJECTION BUCKETS

Salespeople, on the other hand, have a harder time understanding their boundaries. Even though clients routinely raise the same objections, salespeople still struggle to respond appropriately. Over time, an organization should formulate a list of common client objections so they are better equipped to handle them.

Objections fall into a standard set of five buckets.

IN THE DOG HOUSE
Types of objections

LACK OF KNOWLEDGE
- *" We don't need a mobile solution"*
- *Client cannot see the point*
- *These should be discovered early on*
- *Can be countered by case studies or competitor details*

SPECIFIC CONCERN
- *"Your price is too high compared to competitor"*
- *Ask specific questions about what looks too high*
- *Find out what is not required*
- *Apples vs apples comparison?*
- *What specific feature do you need?*

HIDDEN AGENDA
- *Not investing in development of the business case*
- *Explore for history with the competitor*
- *Offer to not bid or leave*
- *Tell customer you are unsure, and ask for their specific input*

PERCEPTION
- *"The cloud isn't secure."*
- *What would the customer need to see or experience?*
- *Do you have third party sites or customer success stories?*

PRICE
- *See chapter 9, "How much is that Doggy in the Window"*

1. The first is the *knowledge* bucket, which means the client doesn't fully understand the benefits of the solution you are offering. For example, a retailer who has been in business for several years might understand that their clients find them through advertisements in the local newspaper. That same retailer may not understand the benefits of creating a mobile-friendly website with an online shopping cart. The person selling those services will run into some challenges because their client lacks the knowledge around how helpful and convenient online tools can be for a retail business.

How to handle a knowledge objection: Share successful case studies or details about previous customers.

2. The client may have a *specific, warranted concern,* such as price or length of time for delivery. For example, a custom deployment often takes several months to install and may even require parts shipped from multiple overseas locations. Specific concerns are often easy to identify and address, based on the individual business. Every industry has its own set of issues. Pool installers are under a time crunch to design and build their clients' pools. Car salespeople might need to wait for a particular make, model, or color to become available.

How to handle a specific, warranted objection: Ask specific questions about what looks too high. Determine what specific part of the solution is required.

3. Occasionally, the client has a *hidden agenda*. Either they have a preference for a different solution, they aren't comfortable discussing the issue, or there's a disconnect on where they see the value. If a client is courting the competition, you have an opportunity to dig deeper with the client and identify an issue you can work with.

How to handle a hidden agenda: Explore the customer's history with the competitor. Tell the customer you're confused or unclear on the issue and hand it back to him or her.

4. One of the biggest obstacles for salespeople lies in the *perception* bucket. For example, a client might say, "I don't want my information stored in the cloud because I don't think it's a secure application." That statement tells you that the client needs further education on how cloud applications work and what it means in terms of security before they are able to make an informed decision. You'll need to enlist the marketing department to provide the client with additional information.

How to handle the perception objection: Ask what the customer would need to see or experience. Bring in third-party success stories.

5. The fifth bucket is when the client is either *not interested* or not clear about his needs. Perhaps he doesn't have the people, time, or resources to move forward, or it is not a top priority.

How to handle the "not interested" objection: Say, "That's okay." Make a note to follow up in the future, and move on. Enlist marketing to keep the client engaged and start the education process.

Client objections will always fall into one of the five core buckets. Businesses need to provide their sales teams with the tools to identify and recognize common objections and instruction on how best to deal with them. Oftentimes, when a salesperson goes through the exercise of identifying the issue, they recognize that the problem could have—and should have—been addressed earlier through better education in the sales process. Typically, the business case has simply not been built.

HANDLING OBJECTIONS

Client objections tend to come late in the process and disrupt momentum. The salesperson may feel dejected, like they've just been sent to the doghouse. There is likely added pressure from management coupled with the anticipation of being in the final stages of the sale. Objections can be soul crushing. The temptation is to rebuke the client, but instead, follow a process to handle the objections.

Don't put yourself in the doghouse and miss out on the sale by focusing on the wrong areas. Take off the blinders and explore potential people, time, or resource issues, which can usually be solved, instead of pressing forward into a danger zone. There are situations where salespeople grind their heels in and try to push the sale through regardless. Perhaps they have seen other clients succeed with the same solution, and they think the business case is painfully obvious.

The last thing you want to do is alienate the client by being too pushy. Don't try to force your own agenda. Instead, accept your client's limitations, and identify what factors influence the final decision.

It's important to recognize that sales can stall for any number of reasons, and there are times when the client may be preoccupied with other matters. Use the constraints as an opportunity to remain engaged with your clients.

I was working with a salesperson recently who shared his frustration toward a client. He was trying to sell an online ordering tool to a pizza-shop owner. The shop owner acknowledged that his business was suffering because he wasn't set up to take orders online. The competition was doing circles around him, he knew he needed the software, but he simply refused to commit. The salesperson could not make heads or tails of the predicament and was annoyed to the point of arguing with the shop owner. Needless to say, the relationship fell apart because the salesperson and the client dug their heels in on opposite sides of the fence.

Later, the salesperson learned the owner was planning to relocate. The client was not in a position to invest the required time commitment to new ordering technology. The cost of the move also put a strain on his finances. Had the salesperson approached the situation with a softer touch and tried to uncover the client's issues, he would have been in a position to reapproach the owner in six or twelve months. Instead, his reflex reaction was to get frustrated, and poof!—there went months of groundwork.

To be proactive in handling objections, arm yourself with the appropriate responses according to which bucket the issue falls in. Even though marketing is responsible for the education piece, salespeople will naturally encounter questions at some point during the sales process.

SAMUEL SAYS: HAVE ANSWERS READY FOR OBJECTIONS.

Common client objections should be widely known, and sales should be prepared with answers. For example, when a client says, "Your price is too high. It's more expensive than we can afford," you need to have a price-objection response ready. An appropriate reply is, "I understand you've been comparing us to some of our competitors in the marketplace, and we expect you to do that. Are there any particular elements of the solution that are more expensive than what you anticipated?" This line of questioning invites the client to relax and open up so that you can uncover the underlying issue.

Handling common client objections often comes down to hearing what the client is really saying. If the client says, "You're a big company," they are *really* saying, "Am I going to get the attention I need to see this project through?" It's important to understand the intent behind their statements, and your own language must be adjusted. To clarify the client's true meaning, use phrases such as these:

- Let me see if I understand.
- Interesting question.
- I'm not sure; let me get the answer for you.
- When you say X, do you mean Y?

Once you've been through the exercise of identifying common objections, either individually or as a team, the new reflex reaction becomes how to tackle them. You're prepared to clarify the client's concerns and redirect them toward a resolution, instead of feeling threatened and defensive. Overcoming objections is easier when you're using a solutions-centered approach, rather than letting the objections become a bone of contention.

In a case where the client needs to be redirected back to marketing, it's important to ask the client for permission to stay in contact. By asking for permission, you are effectively accomplishing two things: you are coming to a mutual agreement that (1) now is not the right time to move forward with the sale and that (2) you will continue to explore the opportunity together at a later time.

Of course, many times the client tells the salesperson, "Now is not a good time. Check back with me in three months." Three months rolls around, the salesperson dutifully follows up with the client, and nothing has changed. To avoid this scenario, the salesperson should carefully examine what is in the way *now*. What are the existing constraints, and what is likely to change in three months? Does the time deferment make sense for both parties? What specific information can marketing share with the client to help him tackle his immediate issues? These are the types of questions that will help to keep you out of the doghouse and enjoy a long-lasting and productive relationship with your clients.

THE OBJECTION-HANDLING FORMULA

All salespeople need to embrace an objection-handling formula. This will help them to avoid problematic areas and prevent them from making the same mistakes repeatedly. Most importantly, it will help them refrain from the reflex of pushing back against the objections. Salespeople tend to follow the same process without realizing they could be overlooking something. It's worth speaking with your peers to get a sense of areas where you might be missing opportunities.

How the salesperson handles objections is an important turning point in his relationship with the client. It's not uncommon to become defensive or frustrated, as my friend did with the pizza-store owner. It's almost a reflex, a gut reaction. Salespeople push back. They try to sell harder, or they throw up their hands in defeat.

However, engaging in a push-pull is not beneficial for either party. When clients hear defensive language, they start to throw up walls. They think you've missed the point and you care only about yourself. To effectively preserve and protect the relationship, the salesperson must suppress the common, knee-jerk reaction and find a way to move forward.

THE OBJECTION-HANDLING FORMULA: HEAR THE CLIENT OUT + SEEK TO UNDERSTAND + WORK TO RESOLVE + CONFIRM RESOLUTION.

The best course of action is to stop, think, and seek to understand where the client is coming from. Your goal is to bring the walls down and figure out a way to deal with the client's objection.

HEAR THE CLIENT OUT

Let the customer talk through the detail of the objection. Don't interrupt and don't rebut. The temptation is to jump in when the customer is partway through describing a scenario, especially if you have heard it before and you've successfully dealt with the objection. It's not personal. It's about what the customer wants and the issues he or she perceives. It's your role to help them work through it.

You don't need to agree or disagree. Simply let the client table the issue in as much detail as possible. If anything, encourage them to go into detail and share hard evidence. Explore what might have brought this issue to the forefront now instead of earlier.

The more background you have on the issue, the better your chances of getting to the root cause and working toward a resolution. Your job is to listen, not try to explain every single issue as it is raised.

UNDERSTAND IT COMPLETELY

The client needs to feel that you have heard and understood their issue. If they think you only have a vague understanding of their concern, they will only expect a vague solution. If the issue is a collection of additional issues rolled into one overall concern, break each component out individually.

If the customer has used some sort of jargon or industry language that could be misinterpreted, spend the time to ensure the terminology is defined. If his objections are centered in soft evidence, seek clarity to find the hard evidence. Resolution needs to be based on a measureable outcome or change.

Open your response with a clarifying statement to demonstrate that you understand the client. For example, "If I understand your concern correctly, you are worried about the time implementation requires and how it will impact your ROI in this year." If the customer is concerned about operational risk, you need to explore what operational risk means to him. Where does he see a potential issue? Without understanding the fine details, you'll be unable to move forward.

Why is the customer feeling the way she does? Do you understand the objection? Do you have hard evidence of the impact of the objection? If the issue remains, how will it show up in the business, and what impact would it have on the final outcome? Keep exploring it. It might seem counterintuitive, but it helps to flush out the problems and gives you something to work with.

WORK TO RESOLVE IT

What does the client need to see or hear to eliminate the objection? Get clarity around exactly what the client needs.

Avoid being swayed by a vague notion that the client might be happy. There needs to be a tangible outcome.

Once you understand what the resolution to the objection is, make sure it is dealt with completely. If a compromise is required, be clear about what it is and work through it. For example, if the customer wants an impossible time frame, be up-front about your limitations. Have a frank and open conversation. Otherwise, the issue will come out again later, when it might be too late to address.

If there are concerns, questions, or issues that you don't have the answer for, tell the customer that you will get back to him. Do not use language such as, "I think so," or "We may be able to." Taking a guess or trying to move forward with uncertainty doesn't work. It destroys trust and confidence. The best way to maintain trust is to simply say, "That's a valid question. I'm not 100 percent certain of the answer. Let me get back to you tomorrow when I have all the information you need." Demonstrate to the client that you will not move forward until his questions are answered and his concerns are resolved.

Above all, ensure that the client's objections have been resolved to his satisfaction. Do not assume. Make sure you have verbal confirmation that the issue is off the table.

GET OBJECTIONS ON THE TABLE EARLY

Often, there are a number of known objections or issues that need to be dealt with during the sales process. Some salespeople have a tendency to gloss over them, but the better course of action is to address them early on in the conversation.

Good wine gets better with age when left in the dark. Customer objections do the opposite. A client with unanswered questions is open to counsel from any source. It could come from people who don't really know or care about the objections. The salesperson needs to get client objections on the table as soon as possible and uncover what the client needs to see and hear to feel comfortable moving forward.

For example, if a client is replacing an older product that has failed, the salesperson needs to address how the product responds over time and with age. Don't sweep problems under the rug. Deal with them right up front.

CORRECT AND DIRECT

People have a natural tendency to correct, direct, or support you. Many times, I found myself in the tender situation of representing the expensive, premium vendor. There were usually other, lower bids on the table. Instead of pretending I was the only game in town, I came right out and acknowledged the other bids. There was no point in wasting everyone's time and ignoring the bids. The trick was to present the conversation in a way that encouraged the client to direct or correct the situation.

Typically, I'd open the conversation by saying, "We are probably among the most expensive options that responded to your tender. I'm sure you will see some very competitive quotes and have a lot to consider." Usually, the client will step in and say something to correct my statement, such as, "We are not looking for the cheapest option. We want to look at the total cost of ownership in terms of ongoing support." That is critical information from the client. He just gave me a strong clue as to where to focus my bid. The client is interested to know how we can differentiate ourselves. Plus, because of this conversation, we are subconsciously positioned differently in the client's mind than the competition.

Don't deny the issue or try to fight potential objections. For example, if you say something like, "We are not as expensive as you might think," you've immediately made the client suspicious of your pricing.

The key is to get the objections out early and state what the customer might interpret. Don't deny the issue or fight the potential objection. If you want to firmly make a point in the client's mind, deny what they think; that will make sure they keep that point of view. Denial has the opposite effect than putting someone's mind at ease.

SALES MEETS PROJECT MANAGEMENT

If your customer is using a committee to select and deploy your solution, alignment between a sales and project management approach is useful. Any solution presented will be evaluated under a number of constraints:

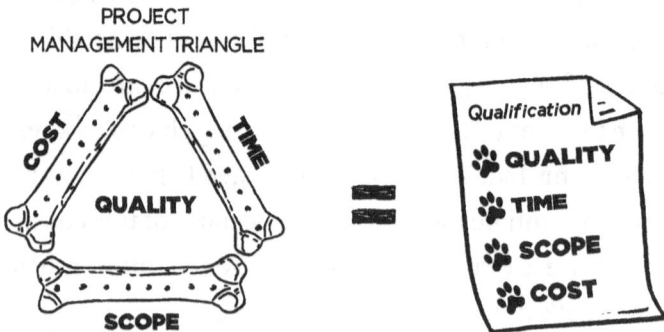

All these factors are interrelated. If one of them is changed, it will affect all the others. In order for the project to be deployed, the business case to be formed, and the ROI and the value of the solution to be properly defined, the sales process needs to work through the triple constraints (also called the Iron Triangle in project management).

The best complex-solution salespeople have a project management mind-set. They properly define the scope, ask the hard questions, gather evidence, and get clarity around responsibilities, capabilities, and timelines.

I learned a lot about solution sales when I completed my project management qualification. In working with the client during the qualifying and quoting stages, I discovered I was also identifying the scope of the project and the quality of the solution. Once the deal was complete, the actual project manager simply created the work breakdown structures to kick off.

If there were client issues, they tended to stem from a lack of clarity around the project scope. Using a project management mentality and the language associated with it in the sales process is a powerful way of pitching. It helps to demonstrate that you are on the client's side because you are viewing the solution from his perspective and considering its impact.

The most powerful application of this approach is in price negotiation. If the customer understands the idea of triple constraints, which most of them do, then she understands how they are all connected. You are able to frame the price conversation in the context of the additional factors.

The conversation simply becomes this:

CUSTOMER: "We are about $100,000 over budget."

SALESPERSON: "What elements of the project can we change that will have a minimal effect on the outcome you are trying to achieve?"

The discussion then looks at what could be achieved with a minimal effect on the desired outcome. Was an element of the project deferred until the next budgetary cycle? Will the project take longer to implement because manpower was reduced? Has the IT investment been impacted? Sometimes the customer simply says, "Can you reduce your rates?"

The end result is a mature and sensible discussion about where the client is prepared to compromise for the sake of price integrity. If you're selling complex business-to-business solutions, understanding the project management discipline is critical. The Project Management Body of Knowledge is a global standard. When both sides are operating within the same framework and language, you have a powerful advantage over other vendors who are simply pushing their approach, without considering the internal impact.

BEST IN SHOW: ARM YOURSELF
WITH ANSWERS

1. Run a brainstorming session to identify the most common objections or concerns (except price).

2. Which of the five buckets does your customer's objection belong in?

3. What objections or concerns could marketing deal with (e.g., knowledge or perception concerns), and what does that resolution look like?

4. What responses and resolutions have worked for those objections?

5. Review whether customer-facing parts of the business are experiencing early client objections.

6. Have you employed a project management mentality to the sales process?

   🏆 What are the time frame, cost, and scope of the project?

CHAPTER 10

IT'S TIME TO STOP BARKING

The vineyard had a little gate in front of the entrance to the driveway that was lined with exotic fruit trees. When the season was right, the neighbors casually drifted over and attempted to pinch some of the delectable, foreign fruits that fell from the trees.

Sam guarded that gate with the same protectiveness that he did the cellar sales. He was only there on the weekends and surprised the neighbor kids that hopped the fence to help themselves to the fruit. They'd find Sam on the other side waiting for them, going bananas. His protective instinct kicked in, and he guarded the property ferociously. The noise and the clamor that ensued forced the kids to retreat empty-handed.

Sometimes, deliveries were left outside the gate or clients showed up after hours. The same thing would happen. Sam would be there, guarding his territory, and start barking. Once he realized that those people weren't a threat, he stopped immediately. He made a quick judgment of the person on the other side of the gate and went from being aggressive to passive. The person would open the gate and come through to find a friendly Sam there, tail wagging, wet ball ready for a throw. In the space of two minutes, Sam went from being a ferocious guard dog, ready to rip someone's leg off, to his usual enthusiastic self.

The same transition occurs in the sales world. As clients get closer to a purchasing decision, salespeople need to assess when to push forward and when to sit quietly. Just like Sam, if you bark too loudly, the clients will run away.

Many salespeople have the tendency to get overly excited when they sense they are nearing a close. They start talking too much. They inadvertently bring potential objections or roadblocks to the client's attention and essentially talk themselves out of the sale. They may think they are providing the client with valuable insight, but in fact, they're giving the client too much information.

I saw this scenario unfold all the time at the vineyard. Someone might have a bottle or two of wine in hand and say, "I think this will go well with the fish I am preparing tonight." Then, the person in sales would say, "Yes, and it will also cellar beautifully for the next ten years."

The salesperson was trying to include an added benefit for the client, but the information was irrelevant to what the client was looking for. It had an adverse effect because then the client said, "You know what? This is actually a little more than I wanted to spend on wine for dinner. It will probably be better if it's cellared for another five years anyway. I'll pass." There went that sale.

BUYING SIGNALS

Typically, when clients are getting close to making a buying decision, they will follow a specific pattern that the salesperson needs to be attuned to. They send off certain buying signals such as asking affirming questions or referring to the product or service in a possessive manner. This is the time for the salesperson to slow down and assist the client in taking ownership.

Let's say the client is considering a kitchen renovation. It takes some time for all the pieces to fall together, to order and manufacture the appliances, and to line up the installation team. The client is usually working toward a specific future event.

For example, they client might want the brand-new, shiny kitchen ready and functional in time to host the family Christmas gathering. In which case, the client will give the salesperson an important clue by saying, "If I choose to move forward with the design by early November, will the kitchen be complete by the second week of December?" Or she might say, "Is it true that the new oven will allow me to cook at a faster rate and hold more dishes?"

These statements indicate the client is validating what they've learned during the sales process. They are confirming the benefits or features they'll receive when they make the purchasing decision. When clients ask future-based questions, they are seriously considering the implications of the offer. It means they are thinking about how their problems will be solved *after* they make the purchase.

SAMUEL SAYS: LISTEN FOR THE CONVERSATION SWAP TO VALIDATION AND OWNERSHIP.

It's also common for the client to revisit topics that have already been discussed in the sales process, such as prerequisites for installation. They'll bring up issues related to risk minimization or transfer. Using the kitchen example again, the client might say, "Do you know someone who will be able to come in and remove all the old appliances and dispose of them?" They'll start to ask questions about warranties or if someone will show them how to use the new equipment. They may even ask questions about returns, such as, "If I'm not happy with my new refrigerator, how much time do I have to return it for a different model?" They're letting the real implications of making a decision gel in their mind.

Validation leads to accepting ownership, which is an important and necessary transition for the client. This is a dangerous time because it's when many salespeople botch the sale. At this point, the client should be doing more of the talking than the salesperson, whose job is to simply affirm that the client understands the process.

The salesperson needs to look for two distinct signals from the client at this stage of the process. If the client is seeking validation, which he or she often is, now is the time to carefully confirm the soundness of the client's decision.

Do not make the mistake of confusing education-related questions with validation, which is a common sales pitfall. For example, early in the sales conversation, the client may ask an education-type question such as, "How does this feature work?" Later, as the client moves toward a purchasing decision, the client may refer to the same feature again. This time, it is put forward as a statement rather than as a question, such as, "So, this feature will allow me to save more time." When clients revisit earlier discussion points to confirm their understanding, they are moving toward validation. The difference between education and validation is subtle and can be deadly. If you confuse the two, you risk clients feeling pushed toward a sale. They'll clam up, and the deal will unravel quickly.

TRANSFER OF OWNERSHIP

There are specific things the salesperson can do to move the client from education to validation to ownership. Each industry has its own method of making the transfer. I've seen some car salespeople allow the client to take the vehicle home for the evening. The idea is that if the client takes his whole family for a ride in it and parks it in the driveway overnight, he will naturally feel more attached to it. It's almost as if he has already bought the car, and it's an effective ownership transfer tactic.

The same thing happens in a shoe store when someone tries on a new pair of shoes. As soon as the client has tried the shoes on and walked around in them for a few minutes, they're already imagining how they will look with a certain outfit. They start to experience how the whole look might work.

At the vineyard, the clients tasted the wine they were considering. We were always busy on weekends at lunchtime in cellar sales. People came in, tried a few different varieties, and I saw them working out in their minds how a certain wine would suit the dinner party they were hosting or attending that night.

After a taste, they often said, "Oh, this would go beautifully with the beef tenderloin I'm serving tonight." As they tasted the wine, they were envisioning how the party would unfold. They saw their friends gathered around the table, drinking beautiful wine, as they told the story of visiting a great vineyard earlier that afternoon to select it. Very rarely did anyone buy an expensive wine without tasting it first.

The validation and transfer of ownership is a critical piece in the sales process, but it's also something that marketing can support in a big way. It's particularly important now that most buyers are 50 percent of the way through the buying decision by the time they even talk to a salesperson. Marketing assists in the process by sharing case studies, test results, white papers, and other valuable market-tested information.

TRANSFER OF OWNERSHIP AND VALIDATION

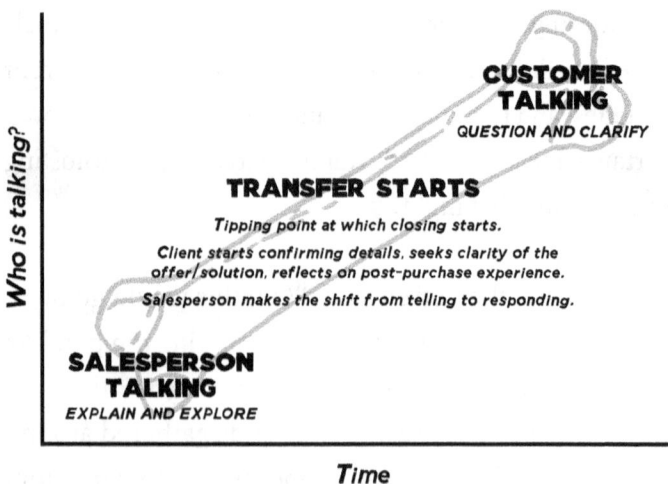

CUSTOMER TALKING
QUESTION AND CLARIFY

TRANSFER STARTS
Tipping point at which closing starts.
Client starts confirming details, seeks clarity of the offer/solution, reflects on post-purchase experience.
Salesperson makes the shift from telling to responding.

SALESPERSON TALKING
EXPLAIN AND EXPLORE

Who is talking? (vertical axis)

Time (horizontal axis)

In a complex software scenario, the marketing team can share success stories of other clients who have implemented the solution and are enjoying its benefits. They have access to tangible change results as well as hard evidence, which allows the client to confirm what they understand. Marketing tools get them in the mind-set of previous clients and validate the benefits.

Our clients at the vineyard often tapped into marketing's educational materials in real time, during tastings. If someone was passionate about wine and trying a new vineyard for the first time, he pulled up the website on the spot. While he swilled the wine in his glass, he could read about tasting notes, food pairings, vintage details for a particular year, and the weather conditions the grapes endured. I may have had a conversation with the client about exactly the same information, but having access to it on the Web provided him with the validation he needed to make the buying decision.

VIRTUAL REALITY

In recent years, virtual reality has become a great way to reduce risk for clients. For example, while wine tasting allows clients to smell and taste the wine, virtual reality lets them see, feel, and hear. The ability to feel is the game changer. Although the headsets and applications are in the early stages, we are less than two years away from virtual reality becoming part of the marketing mix. Any company that sells high-involvement, high-investment solutions in the consumer and business marketplace will use virtual reality.

It's an effective tool when the decision has:

- A number of stakeholders
- Consequences for several years
- A big financial investment
- An impact on the surroundings (i.e., seeing it in context is meaningful)

Virtual reality achieves a number of key hurdles in the sales process because it reduces risk and helps with the transfer of ownership. Several real-estate companies are using it to show premium office and retail space. The prospective tenant is able to "walk" around the space, take in the views, get a sense of the natural light, and most importantly, get a "real" sense of the property. Furthermore, multiple stakeholders can all experience the same thing and tackle their own individual concerns.

In the consumer space, a landscaper or kitchen renovator has a serious advantage if he can offer the client an opportunity to experience exactly what the end result will look like. The decision shifts from cost and confidence in the supplier to one that demonstrates the final solution.

CLOSING THE DEAL

Throughout the sales conversation, you've worked hard with the client to make sure the purchase makes sense. You've flushed out the client's concerns and addressed any issues that may stop the purchase from proceeding. You have also clearly established what problem the client is trying to solve or the benefit he or she is trying to gain. Now it's time to move toward a "trial close"—the purpose of which is to establish if the client is ready to seal the deal.

When using the trial close, the client is 80-90 percent of the way through the sales process. They have already started to ask validating questions and speak in future terms, and they are very close to pulling the trigger. To understand if the client is truly ready and ensure that you've addressed all the outstanding issues, listen closely for the conversation swap and adhere to the following checklist.

TRIAL CLOSE FORMULA

1. Restate the agreed value, how your solution solves the client's problem, and what the return on investment will be.
2. Repeat the offer: "For XYZ price, we will have the product delivered to you by PDQ date. You will be enjoying the benefits within the first six weeks after the install date."
3. Ask for the order: "Does next Wednesday work for delivery of the order?"
4. Shut up!

At this stage in the deal, it is vital that the salesperson says nothing. Let "the ask" hang in silence. Do not try to drive the conversation or start sharing unnecessary information. Just sit there and shut up. The client will do one of two things. They will either agree outright or they will raise additional objections. If the latter is the case, address the objections with the same level of patience and understanding that you have throughout the sales cycle.

As you near the finish line, there is a magic moment when the client starts using ownership language in relation to the product or service. It's a very subtle shift, but one of the leading signs is when the client takes over the conversation. It's exactly like when Sam made a quick and internal decision that the person on the other side of the gate was okay to let through. If you are a well-trained salesperson skilled in the fine art of listening, you'll know when the client is prepared to cross the threshold and move forward with the deal. You'll feel it on an instinctual level, so stop barking!

YES COMES IN THREE FLAVORS

As salespeople, we are taught to do everything we possibly can to get the client to say yes. The second we hear that magic word, we move on as quickly as we can to make sure the client doesn't change their mind, which has been known to happen.

On a number of occasions, as soon as I heard those magic words, I scurried back to my own office to assemble the project team. I felt like a hero who had just created work for all the people on my team and that I had contributed to the company's sales targets. But on just as many occasions, the project manager arrived and started to scope the job. The process brought up several issues, and suddenly the client couldn't or wouldn't execute the basic requirements to get the job started. Even worse, sometimes the client did nothing, until we finally realized the project wasn't going anywhere. We had nothing more than hope.

"Yes" comes in three flavors, and the only one that counts is the one that results in a commitment to execute. From working with project managers, I learned that the process of defining tasks and actions helped the client identify what they needed to do on their end. If they were unable to execute, the sale was going nowhere. A yes from a client needs to be accompanied with a clear action plan. Without the customer knowing *how* and *when* he is going to implement the solution, the original yes is worthless.

Consider the stories of people who live generally unhealthy lifestyles, and their doctors tell them they have to change their ways. The unhealthy person says, "Yes, Doc. I hear you. I'm on it. I'll change my ways." The patient acknowledges the need to change and sometimes even sounds enthusiastic. The minute he steps out of the doctor's office, he lights up a cigarette and stops at McDonald's for lunch. Although the patient agreed to change his ways, the *how* and *when* were not pinned down.

The same scenario can unfold with clients who say yes. It's a well-intentioned yes, but they don't have a way forward, which can kill the deal. Saying yes is just the start; it's not the result. There must be a commitment to action, which can only come from an understanding of the *how* and the *when*. It's tempting to brush over that level of planning and hope that everything will sort itself out in due course. An agreement means a sale, and you likely want to celebrate instead of focus on the small details.

However, if your client has a detailed procurement process or needs to develop a business case, and neither of those steps have occurred, the yes you have is nothing more than a well-meaning intention.

More and more, the sales process overlaps with project management, especially in large, complex organizations. If you heard your client say yes, make sure you know which flavor of yes it is.

1. No way.

The client said yes, but she really wanted to say no. She may feel trapped, or she wants to keep playing fetch. Or the other stakeholders have said no, and your client doesn't want to tell you the truth. She uses yes as a stall tactic. She goes silent. The sale is abandoned when the client stops answering the phone.

2. Don't know.

The client said yes, but he doesn't know how to execute. Maybe he doesn't have the authority to execute. He said yes prematurely. It's likely the client still has considerable work to do before he can move forward.

3. Now.

The client said yes, and they have time-bound deliverables. This is the yes you want! They have clear action items to execute against. The business case is clear, as are the resources and the timeline. The customer understands how and when to take action. You prepare an invoice.

Some salespeople have it drilled into them that the only outcome that matters is a yes. They're taught silly question patterns. Think of a telemarketer, who calls and asks, "Do you like to save money?" The client says yes. "Do you think your utilities bill is too high?" Again, the client says yes. Then the telemarketer says, "Are you available at 6:00 p.m. tomorrow night for our sales representative to stop by and show you how other people in your neighborhood have saved 30 percent on their bills?" The telemarketer is waiting for the automatic yes that the client has been primed for. But the client is ready for it. He knows the routine, and he's defensive. He feels as if he's being sold to, because he is. Although the client might say yes, he's not likely to answer the door when the representative comes around or say yes in the meeting.

Make sure that you have the right yes. Yes without the client understanding how and when to take action is worthless. Don't be afraid of a genuine no. It allows you to uncover the real issues and objections. A no gives you the opportunity to ask the client what they need to hear, see, or do to proceed. It flushes out objections, so that you can move to a real yes, now.

BEST IN SHOW: MOVING THE SALE FORWARD

1. **How can you help the transfer of ownership process?**

   🏆 Take whatever action is necessary to help clients feel that they are enjoying the benefits of the solution. Let them take the car for a drive, for example.

   🏆 Are "sample" or "demonstration" versions of your product an option?

   🏆 What new technology options (such as virtual reality) would assist with the transfer of ownership?

2. **What are the validation signs?**

   🏆 Do your customers ask the same validation questions repeatedly or in a different way? That is, do they keep dwelling on the same issue?

   🏆 Brainstorm the three most common validation questions your clients ask. Do you have a well-polished response and clear transition to a trial close?

3. **What are the typical post purchase scenarios in your business?**

   🏆 Build a list of client benefits to address closing questions on the fly.

4. **How will you close the deal? Do you know the flavor of your client's yes?**

CONCLUSION

The purpose of this book is to recognize the massive changes affecting sales and marketing as a result of technology. Inside, I've provided professionals within those fields the tools to succeed in the modern world.

In the old days, salespeople were responsible for educating clients on the benefits of their products and services. Today, with the wide availability of information and third-party reviews, clients are largely self-educated. They show up on the doorstep already halfway through their decision process.

The four principles of marketing from yesteryear—place, promotion, product, and price—have been replaced by data-driven, Internet-user behavioral science. There used to be an old joke in marketing: Our spend works; we're just not sure which half. Now marketing is just as accountable for dollars as sales. The playing field has been leveled.

We're no longer measuring client cycles in months or quarters. Often marketing initiatives and response are measured by days, if not hours, and plans are modified accordingly. Salespeople have become an expensive resource. They are well educated in the solutions they are selling, and the use of their time needs to be carefully allocated. Although the marketing team has absorbed their education responsibilities, they are now required to understand and align themselves with the decision process and the multiple stakeholders that make a final decision. Sales is more about decision enablement than persuasion.

Sales and marketing need to work closely together to deliver the same message, ensure client engagement, and understand the client's needs. It's not about the final sales push; it's about the client's journey and their relationship with the company from beginning to end.

The salesperson and the client have to be equally invested in the sales process for a successful outcome to occur. If either party is vague about the issues or unclear on the desired results, the sale will falter. Therefore, the salesperson must be an integral part of helping the client build a business case and understand all the dynamics—internal and external—that could impact the sale.

The sales process is anchored in exploring the clients' issues from their perspective. Salespeople need to adopt a project management approach and define the scope of the endeavor, ask the obvious and not-so-obvious questions, uncover the constraints, and dive into the complexities of the solution. The scoping exercise is closely aligned with the qualification process in that both pursuits identify what needs to be achieved, the resources available, and the time frame in which it needs to happen.

Success on the shared journey with the client will depend largely on several factors:

- How well you understand you clients' needs
- How adeptly you engage with the clients throughout the sales process
- How many resources you have in terms of alliances with other professionals related to your industry (your pack)
- How organized your own schedule is
- How realistic you are about whether a sale is or is not going to happen and what to do about it

Although this book is packed with methods and techniques to work with risk-averse clients, the salesperson's true intentions are paramount. Even the best strategies will only get you so far. If you are not genuinely focused on providing your clients with real solutions to their immediate and long-term problems, they'll look elsewhere. Today's clients are looking for partners and allies, not product pushers.

Our beloved mongrel mutt, Sam, was endearing to people near and far because of his genuine intent. It was quite easy to tell when he was in playful mode or when he was in guard-dog mode. The same is true in business. Clients will always be able to get a read on a salesperson's true motivation. Are you helping to solve a problem, or are you simply trying to close a deal?

Be like Sam. Get out there and engage with your clients. Bring your authenticity and enthusiasm to the table every day, and the clients will line up to play ball.

ACKNOWLEDGMENTS

Thanks to my dad, Kevin. You showed me that sales and marketing is a rewarding profession in so many ways. Plus, you showed me that working at it and grinding away gets it done.

Thanks to Evan, who continues to guide me in growing and developing a business. Thank you for the good times we've enjoyed and, more importantly, for your assistance through the tough times when you steered a way through.

Thanks, Google.

ABOUT THE AUTHOR

STEVE DE MAMIEL is old enough to remember when sales and marketing was footwork and phone calls, and young enough to have seen technology make his marketing degree worthless. He received his Bachelor of Business from Edith Cowan University in Perth, Western Australia, and then moved to Sydney to open an office for a small systems integrator. Steve learned the hard way that the only way to win against competing global companies was to stop selling and start solving. He has led a number of companies through successful evolutions and is a keen study of changing industry trends. He lives in Melbourne where he brings sales and marketing training to life in a memorable way.

www.ingramcontent.com/pod-product-compliance
Lightning Source LLC
Chambersburg PA
CBHW070926210326
41520CB00021B/6821